THEORIES OF
PRIMITIVE RELIGION

THEORIES OF
PRIMITIVE RELIGION

BY

E. E. EVANS-PRITCHARD

PROFESSOR OF SOCIAL ANTHROPOLOGY
IN THE UNIVERSITY OF OXFORD

OXFORD
AT THE CLARENDON PRESS

Oxford University Press, Ely House, London W. 1

GLASGOW NEW YORK TORONTO MELBOURNE WELLINGTON
CAPE TOWN SALISBURY IBADAN NAIROBI LUSAKA ADDIS ABABA
BOMBAY CALCUTTA MADRAS KARACHI LAHORE DACCA
KUALA LUMPUR HONG KONG TOKYO

FIRST PUBLISHED 1965

REPRINTED LITHOGRAPHICALLY IN GREAT BRITAIN
AT THE UNIVERSITY PRESS, OXFORD
FROM CORRECTED SHEETS OF THE FIRST EDITION
BY VIVIAN RIDLER
PRINTER TO THE UNIVERSITY
1966, 1967

FOREWORD

FOUR of these Sir D. Owen Evans Lectures were delivered at the University College of Wales, Aberystwyth, in the spring of 1962. They are presented almost entirely as written for that occasion, though some paragraphs were not spoken because the lectures would otherwise have exceeded the time allotted to me. The Lecture appearing as no. IV here was written at the same time, but as I was asked to give only four lectures, it was not delivered.

It will be appreciated that these lectures were for the ear and not for the eye; and also that they were spoken to a highly educated, but none the less a non-specialist, that is, non-anthropological, audience. Had I been speaking to professional colleagues or even to anthropological students, I would sometimes have expressed myself in somewhat different language, though to the same import.

In my comments on Tylor and Frazer, Lévy-Bruhl, and Pareto I have drawn heavily on articles published very many years ago in the *Bulletin of the Faculty of Arts*, Egyptian University (Cairo), in which I once held the Chair of Sociology—articles which have circulated between then and now in departments of Social Anthropology in a mimeographed form, and the main points of which are here set forth.

For criticism and advice I thank Dr. R. G. Lienhardt, Dr. J. H. M. Beattie, Dr. R. Needham, Dr. B. R. Wilson, and Mr. M. D. McLeod.

E. E. E.-P.

CONTENTS

I

INTRODUCTION

THESE lectures examine the manner in which various writers who can be regarded as anthropologists, or at any rate as writing in the anthropological field, have attempted to understand and account for the religious beliefs and practices of primitive peoples. I should make it clear at the outset that I shall be primarily concerned only with theories about the religions of primitive peoples. More general discussions about religion outside those limits are peripheral to my subject. I shall therefore keep to what may broadly be considered to be anthropological writings, and for the most part to British writers. You will note that our present interest is less in primitive religions than in the various theories which have been put forward purporting to offer an explanation of them.

If anyone were to ask what interest the religions of the simpler peoples can have for us, I would reply in the first place that some of the most important political, social, and moral philosophers from Hobbes, Locke, and Rousseau to Herbert Spencer, Durkheim, and Bergson have considered the facts of primitive life to have great significance for the understanding of social life in general; and I would remark further that the men who have been most responsible for changing the whole climate of thought in our civilization during the last century, the great myth-makers Darwin, Marx-Engels, Freud, and Frazer (and perhaps I should add Comte), all showed an intense interest in primitive peoples and used what was known about them in their endeavours to convince us that, though what had given solace and encouragement in the past could do so no more, all was not lost; seen down the vistas of history the struggle did avail.

In the second place, I would reply that primitive religions are species of the genus religion, and that all who have any interest in religion must acknowledge that a study of the religious ideas and practices of primitive peoples, which are of great variety, may help us to reach certain conclusions about the nature of religion in general, and therefore also about the so-called higher religions or historical and positive religions or the religions of revelation, including our own. Unlike these higher religions, which are genetically related— Judaism, Christianity, and Islam, or Hinduism, Buddhism, and Jainism—primitive religions in isolated and widely separated parts of the world can scarcely be other than independent developments without historical relations between them, so they provide all the more valuable data for a comparative analysis aiming at determining the essential characteristics of religious phenomena and making general, valid, and significant statements about them.

I am of course aware that theologians, classical historians, Semitic scholars, and other students of religion often ignore primitive religions as being of little account, but I take comfort in the reflection that less than a hundred years ago Max Müller was battling against the same complacently entrenched forces for the recognition of the languages and religions of India and China as important for an understanding of language and religion in general, a fight which it is true has yet to be won (where are the departments of comparative linguistics and comparative religion in this country?), but in which some advance has been made. Indeed I would go further and say that, to understand fully the nature of revealed religion, we have to understand the nature of so-called natural religion, for nothing could have been revealed about anything if men had not already had an idea about that thing. Or rather, perhaps we should say, the dichotomy between natural and revealed religion is false and makes for obscurity, for there is a good sense in which it may be said that all religions are religions of revelation: the world around them and their reason have everywhere revealed to men something of the divine and of their own nature and destiny. We might ponder the words of St. Augustine: 'What is now called the Christian religion, has existed among the ancients, and was not absent from the beginning of the human race, until Christ came in the flesh: from which time the true religion, which existed already, began to be called Christian.'[1]

I have no hesitation in claiming furthermore that though students of the higher religions may sometimes look down their noses at us anthropologists and our primitive religions—we have no texts—it is we more than anyone who have brought together the vast material on a study of which the science of comparative religion has been, however insecurely, founded; and, however inadequate the anthropological theories based on it may be, they could serve, and sometimes have served, classical, Semitic, and Indo-European scholars, and also Egyptologists in the interpretation of their texts. We shall be reviewing some of these theories in the course of these lectures, so I may here merely say that I have in mind the impact on many learned disciplines of the writings of Tylor and Frazer in this country and of Durkheim, Hubert and Mauss, and Lévy-Bruhl in France. We may not today find them acceptable, but in their time they have played an important part in the history of thought.

It is not easy to define what we are to understand by religion for the purpose of these lectures. Were their emphasis to be on beliefs and practices, we might well accept initially Sir Edward Tylor's minimum definition of religion (though there are difficulties attached to it) as belief in spiritual beings, but since the emphasis is rather on theories of primitive religion, I am not free to choose one definition rather than another, since I have to discuss a number of hypotheses which go beyond Tylor's minimum definition. Some would include under the religious rubric such topics as magic, totemism, taboo, and even witchcraft—everything, that is, which may be covered by the expression 'primitive mentality' or what to the European scholar has appeared to be irrational or superstitious. I shall have in particular to make repeated references to magic, because several influential writers do not differentiate between magic and religion and speak of the magico-religious, or regard them as genetically related in an evolutionary development; others again,

---

[1] August. *Retr.* i. 13. Quóted in F. M. Müller, *Selected Essays on Language, Mythology and Religion*, 1881, i. 5.

whilst distinguishing between them, give a similar type of explanation of both.

Victorian and Edwardian scholars were intensely interested in religions of rude peoples, largely, I suppose, because they faced a crisis in their own; and many books and articles have been written on the subject. Indeed, were I to refer to all their authors, these lectures would be clogged with a recitation of names and titles. The alternative I shall adopt is to select those writers who have been most influential or who are most characteristic of one or other way of analysing the facts, and discuss their theories as representative of varieties of anthropological thought. What may be lost by this procedure in detailed treatment is compensated for by greater clarity.

Theories of primitive religion may conveniently be considered under the headings of psychological and sociological, the psychological being further divided into—and here I use Wilhelm Schmidt's terms—intellectualist and emotionalist theories. This classification, which also accords roughly with historical succession, will serve its expository purpose, though some writers fall between these headings or come under more than one of them.

My treatment of them may seem to you severe and negative. I think you will not regard my strictures as too severe when you see how inadequate, even ludicrous, is much of what has been written in explanation of religious phenomena. Laymen may not be aware that most of what has been written in the past, and with some assurance, and is still trotted out in colleges and universities, about animism, totemism, magic, &c., has been shown to be erroneous or at least dubious. My task has therefore to be critical rather than constructive, to show why theories at one time accepted are unsupportable and had, or have, to be rejected wholly or in part. If I can persuade you that much is still very uncertain and obscure, my labour will not have been in vain. You will then not be under any illusion that we have final answers to the questions posed.

Indeed, looking backwards, it is sometimes difficult to understand how many of the theories put forward to account

for primitive man's beliefs and for the origin and development of religion could ever have been propounded. It is not
just that we now know in the light of modern research what
their authors could not then have known. That, of course, is
true; but even on the facts available to them it is astounding
that so much could have been written which appears to be
contrary to common sense. Yet these men were scholars and
of great learning and ability. To comprehend what now seem
to be obviously faulty interpretations and explanations, we
would have to write a treatise on the climate of thought of
their time, the intellectual circumstances which set bounds
to their thought, a curious mixture of positivism, evolution-
ism, and the remains of a sentimental religiosity. We shall be
surveying some of these theories in later lectures, but I should
like here and now to commend to you as a *locus classicus* the
at-one-time widely read and influential *Introduction to the
History of Religion* by F. B. Jevons, then (1896) a teacher of
philosophy in the University of Durham. Religion for him
was a uniform evolutionary development from totemism—
animism being 'rather a primitive philosophical theory than
a form of religious belief'[1]—to polytheism to monotheism;
but I do not intend to discuss, or disentangle, his theories.
I only instance the book as the best example I know for
illustrating how erroneous theories about primitive religions
can be, for I believe it would be true to say that there is no
general, or theoretical, statement about them in it which
would pass muster today. It is a collection of absurd reconstructions, unsupportable hypotheses and conjectures, wild
speculations, suppositions and assumptions, inappropriate
analogies, misunderstandings and misinterpretations, and,
especially in what he wrote about totemism, just plain nonsense.

If some of the theories put before you appear rather naïve,
I would ask you to bear certain facts in mind. Anthropology
was still in its infancy—it has hardly yet grown up. Till
recently it has been the happy hunting ground of men of
letters and has been speculative and philosophical in a rather
old-fashioned way. If psychology can be said to have taken

[1] F. B. Jevons, *An Introduction to the History of Religion*, 1896, p. 206.

the first steps towards scientific autonomy round about 1860 and not to have rid itself of the trammels of its philosophical past till forty or fifty years later, social anthropology, which took its first steps at about the same time, has yet more recently shed similar encumbrances.

It is a remarkable fact that none of the anthropologists whose theories about primitive religion have been most influential had ever been near a primitive people. It is as though a chemist had never thought it necessary to enter a laboratory. They had consequently to rely for their information on what European explorers, missionaries, administrators, and traders told them. Now, I want to make it clear that this evidence is highly suspect. I do not say that it was fabricated, though sometimes it was; and even such famous travellers as Livingstone, Schweinfurth, and Palgrave were given to gross carelessness. But much of it was false and almost all of it was unreliable and, by modern standards of professional research, casual, superficial, out of perspective, out of context; and to some extent this was true even of the earlier professional anthropologists. I say with the greatest deliberation about early descriptions of the simpler peoples' ideas and behaviour, and even more of the interpretations of them put forward, that statements cannot be taken at their face value and should not be accepted without critical examination of their sources and without weighty corroborative evidence.

Anyone who has done research among primitive peoples earlier visited by explorers and others can bear witness that their reports are only too often unreliable, even about matters which can be noted by bare observation, while about such matters as religious beliefs which cannot be so noted their statements may be quite untrue. I give a single example from a region with which I am well acquainted. In view of recent papers and extensive monographs on the religions of the Northern Nilotes, it is strange to read what the famous explorer Sir Samuel Baker said about them in an address to the Ethnological Society of London in 1866: 'Without any exception, they are without a belief in a Supreme Being, neither have they any form of worship or idolatry; nor is the darkness of their minds enlightened by even a ray of superstition. The mind is as stagnant as the morass which forms its puny world.'[1] As early as 1871 Sir Edward Tylor was able to show from the evidence even then available that this could not be true.[2] Statements about a people's religious beliefs must always be treated with the greatest caution, for we are then dealing with what neither European nor native can directly observe, with conceptions, images, words, which require for understanding a thorough knowledge of a people's language and also an awareness of the entire system of ideas of which any particular belief is part, for it may be meaningless when divorced from the set of beliefs and practices to which it belongs. Very rarely could it be said that in addition to these qualifications the observer had a scientific habit of mind. It is true that some missionaries were well educated men and had learnt to speak native languages with fluency, but speaking a language fluently is very different from understanding it, as I have often observed in converse between Europeans and Africans and Arabs. For here there is a new cause of misunderstanding, a fresh hazard. Native and missionary are using the same words but the connotations are different, they carry different loads of meaning. For someone who has not made an intensive study of native institutions, habits, and customs in the native's own milieu (that is, well away from administrative, missionary, and trading posts) at best there can emerge a sort of middle dialect in which it is possible to communicate about matters of common experience and interest. We need only take for example the use of a native word for our 'God'. The meaning of the word for the native speaker may have only the slightest coincidence, and in a very restricted context, with the missionary's conception of God. The late Professor Hocart cites an actual example of such misunderstandings, from Fiji:

When the missionary speaks of God as *ndina*, he means that all other gods are non-existent. The native understands that He is the only effective, reliable god; the others may be effective at

[1] S. W. Baker, 'The Races of the Nile Basin', *Transactions of the Ethnological Society of London*, n.s. v (1867), 231.

[2] E. B. Tylor, *Primitive Culture*, 3rd edit. (1891), i. 423–4.

times, but are not to be depended upon. This is but one example
of how the teacher may mean one thing and his pupil understand
another. Generally the two parties continue blissfully ignorant of
the misunderstanding. There is no remedy for it, except in the
missionary acquiring a thorough knowledge of native customs
and beliefs.[1]

Furthermore, the reports used by scholars to illustrate
their theories were not only highly inadequate but—and
this is what chiefly relates to the topic of these lectures—
they were also highly selective. What travellers liked to put
on paper was what most struck them as curious, crude, and
sensational. Magic, barbaric religious rites, superstitious
beliefs, took precedence over the daily empirical, humdrum
routines which comprise nine-tenths of the life of primitive man and are his chief interest and concern: his hunting
and fishing and collecting of roots and fruits, his cultivating
and herding, his building, his fashioning of tools and
weapons, and in general his occupation in his daily affairs,
domestic and public. These were not allotted the space they
fill, in both time and importance, in the lives of those whose
way of life was being described. Consequently, by giving
undue attention to what they regarded as curious superstitions, the occult and mysterious, observers tended to paint
a picture in which the mystical (in Lévy-Bruhl's sense of
that word) took up a far greater portion of the canvas than
it has in the lives of primitive peoples, so that the empirical, the ordinary, the common-sense, the workaday world
seemed to have only a secondary importance, and the natives
were made to look childish and in obvious need of fatherly
administration and missionary zeal, especially if there was
a welcome bit of obscenity in their rites.

Then the scholars got to work on the pieces of information
provided for them haphazardly and from all over the world,
and built them into books with such picturesque titles as
The Golden Bough and *The Mystic Rose*. These books presented
a composite image, or rather caricature, of the primitive mind:
superstitious, childlike, incapable of either critical or sustained
thought. Examples of this procedure, this promiscuous use

---

[1] A. M. Hocart, 'Mana', *Man*, 1914, 46.

of evidence, might be culled from any writer of the period: thus

The Amaxosa drink the gall of an ox to make themselves fierce. The notorious Mantuana drank the gall of thirty chiefs, believing it would render him strong. Many peoples, for instance the Yorubas, believe that the 'blood is the life'. The New Caledonians eat slain enemies to acquire courage and strength. The flesh of a slain enemy is eaten in Timorlaut to cure impotence. The people of Halmahera drink the blood of slain enemies in order to become brave. In Amboina, warriors drink the blood of enemies they have killed to acquire their courage. The people of Celebes drink the blood of enemies to make themselves strong. The natives of the Dieri and neighbouring tribes will eat a man and drink his blood in order to acquire his strength; the fat is rubbed on sick people.[1]

And so on and on and on through volume after volume.

How well was this procedure satirized by Malinowski, to whom must·go much of the credit for having outmoded by ridicule and example both the sort of inquiries which had previously been prosecuted among the simpler peoples and the use scholars had made of them. He speaks of 'the lengthy litanies of threaded statement, which make us anthropologists feel silly and the savage look ridiculous', such as 'Among the Brobdignacians [*sic*] when a man meets his mother-in-law, the two abuse each other and each retires with a black eye'; 'When a Brodiag encounters a polar bear he runs away and sometimes the bear follows'; 'In old Caledonia when a native accidentally finds a whisky bottle by the road-side he empties it at one gulp, after which he proceeds immediately to look for another.'[2]

We have observed that selection on the level of bare observation had already produced an initial distortion. The scissors-and-paste method of compilation by the armchair scholars at home led to further distortion. On the whole, they lacked any sense of historical criticism, the rules an historian applies when evaluating documentary evidence. Then, if a false impression was created by observers of primitive peoples giving undue prominence to the mystical in their lives, it was

[1] A. E. Crawley, *The Mystic Rose*, 1927 edit. (revised and enlarged by Theodore Besterman), i. 134–5.

[2] B. Malinowski, *Crime and Custom in Savage Society*, 1926, p. 126.

embossed by scrap-book treatment, which was dignified by being labelled the 'comparative method'. This consisted, with respect to our subject, of taking from the first-hand records about primitive peoples, and willy-nilly from all over the world, wrenching the facts yet further from their contexts, only what referred to the strange, weird, mystical, super-stitious—use which words we may—and piecing the bits together in a monstrous mosaic, which was supposed to por-tray the mind of primitive man. Primitive man was thus made to appear, especially in Lévy-Bruhl's earlier books, as quite irrational (in the usual sense of that word), living in a mysterious world of doubts and fears, in terror of the super-natural and ceaselessly occupied in coping with it. Such a picture, I think any anthropologist of today would agree, is a total distortion.

As a matter of fact, the 'comparative method' when so used is a misnomer. There was precious little comparison, if we mean analytical comparison. There was merely a bringing together of items which appeared to have something in common. We can indeed say for it that it enabled the writers to make preliminary classifications in which vast numbers of observations could be placed under a limited number of rubrics, thereby introducing some sort of order; and in this it had value. But it was an illustrative rather than a compara-tive method, almost what psychologists used to call the 'anecdotal method'. A large number of miscellaneous exam-ples were brought together to illustrate some general idea and in support of the author's thesis about that idea. There was no attempt to test theories by unselected examples. The most elementary precautions were neglected as wild surmise followed on wild surmise (called hypotheses). The simplest rules of inductive logic (methods of agreement, difference, and concomitant variations) were ignored. Thus, to give a single example, if God is, as Freud would have it, a projec-tion of the idealized and sublimated image of the father, then clearly it is necessary to show that conceptions of deities vary with the very different places the father has in the family in different types of society. Then again, negative instances, if considered at all, which was rare, were dismissed as later developments, decadence, survivals, or by some other evolutionary trick. For early anthropological theories, as you will see in my next lecture, not only sought explanations of primitive religion in psychological origins, but also attempted to place it in an evolutionary gradation or as a stage in social development. A chain of logical development was deductively constructed. In the absence of historical records it could not be said with any conviction that in any particular instance historical development corresponded to the logical paradigm—indeed from the middle of last century there raged a battle between those in favour of the theory of progression and those in favour of the theory of degradation, the former holding that primitive societies were in a state of early and, retarded though it might be, progressive development towards civilization, and the latter that they had once been in a more highly civilized condition and had regressed from it. The debate especially concerned religion, it being held by the one party that what they considered to be rather elevated theological ideas found among some primitive peoples were a first glimpse of truth that would eventually lead to higher things, and by the other party that those beliefs were a relic of an earlier and more civilized state. Herbert Spencer preserved an open mind on this issue,[1] but the other anthropologists, except Andrew Lang and to some extent Max Müller, and sociologists were progressionists. In the absence of historical evidence to show the phases rude societies have in fact passed through, they were assumed to be of an ascending, and very often an invariable, order. All that was required was to find an example somewhere, no matter where, which more or less corresponded to one or other stage of logical development and to insert it as an illustration, or as the writers seemed to regard it, as proof, of the historical validity of this or that scheme of unilinear progression. Were I addressing a purely anthropological audience, even to allude to such past procedures might be regarded as flogging dead horses.

The difficulties were, I believe, increased, and the resultant distortion made greater, by the coining of special terms to describe primitive religions, thereby suggesting that the mind

[1] H. Spencer, *The Principles of Sociology*, 1882, i. 106.

of the primitive was so different from ours that its ideas could not be expressed in our vocabularies and categories. Primitive religion was 'animism', 'pre-animism', 'fetishism', and the like. Or, terms were taken over from native languages, as though none could be found in our own language resembling what had to be described, such terms as *taboo* (from Polynesia), *mana* (from Melanesia), *totem* (from the Indians of North America), and *baraka* (from the Arabs of North Africa). I am not denying that the semantic difficulties in translation are great. They are considerable enough between, shall we say, French and English; but when some primitive language has to be rendered into our own tongue they are, and for obvious reasons, much more formidable. They are in fact the major problem we are confronted with in the subject we are discussing, so I hope I may be allowed to pursue the matter a little further. If an ethnographer says that in the language of a Central African people the word *ango* means dog, he would be entirely correct, but he has only to a very limited degree thereby conveyed the meaning of *ango*, for what it means to the natives who use the word is very different to what 'dog' means to an Englishman. The significance dogs have for them—they hunt with them, they eat them, and so on—is not the significance they have for us. How much greater is the displacement likely to be when we come to terms which have a metaphysical reference! One can, as has been done, use native words and then demonstrate their meaning by their use in different contexts and situations. But there is clearly a limit to this expedient. Reduced to an absurdity it would mean writing an account of a people in their own vernacular. The alternatives are perilous. One can standardize a word taken from a primitive vernacular, like *totem*, and use it to describe phenomena among other peoples which resemble what it refers to in its original home; but this can be the cause of great confusion, because the resemblances may be superficial, and the phenomena in question so diversified that the term loses all meaning, which, indeed, as Goldenweiser showed,[1] has been the fate of the word *totem*.

[1] A. A. Goldenweiser, *Early Civilization*, 1921, pp. 282 ff. See also his paper 'Form and Content in Totemism', *American Anthropologist*, N.S. xx (1918).

I emphasize this predicament because it has some importance for an understanding of theories of primitive religion. One may, indeed, find some word or phrase in one's own language by which to translate a native concept. We may translate some word of theirs by 'god' or 'spirit' or 'soul' or 'ghost', but then we have to ask not only what the word we so translate means to the natives but also what the word by which it is translated means to the translator and his readers. We have to determine a double meaning; and at best there can be no more than a partial overlap of meaning between the two words.

The semantic difficulties are always considerable and can only be partially overcome. The problem they present may be viewed also in reverse, in the attempt by missionaries to translate the Bible into native tongues. It was bad enough when Greek metaphysical concepts had to be expressed in Latin, and, as we know, misunderstandings arose from this transportation of concepts from the one language into the other. Then the Bible was translated into various other European languages, English, French, German, Italian, &c., and I have found it an illuminating experiment to take some portion of it, shall we say a Psalm, and see how these different languages have stamped it with their particular characters. Those who know Hebrew or some other Semitic language can complete the game by then translating these versions back into its idiom and seeing what they look like then.

How much more desperate is the case of primitive languages! I have read somewhere of the predicament of missionaries to the Eskimoes in trying to render into their tongue the word 'lamb', as in the sentence 'Feed my lambs'. You can, of course, render it by reference to some animal with which the Eskimoes are acquainted, by saying, for instance, 'Feed my seals', but clearly if you do so you replace the representation of what a lamb was for a Hebrew shepherd by that of what a seal may be to an Eskimo. How is one to convey the meaning of the statement that the horses of the Egyptians 'are flesh and not spirit' to a people which has never seen a horse or anything like one, and may also have no concept corresponding to the Hebrew conception of

spirit? These are trite examples. May I give two more complicated ones? How do you translate into Hottentot 'Though
I speak with the tongues of men and of angels and have not
charity . . .'? In the first place, you have to determine what
the passage meant to St. Paul's hearers; and, apart from 'the
tongues of men and of angels', what exegetical learning has
gone to the elucidation of *eros*, *agape*, and *caritas*! Then you
have to find equivalents in Hottentot, and, since there are
none, you do the best you can. Or how do you render into
an Amerindian language 'In the beginning was the word'?
Even in its English form the meaning can only be set forth
by a theological disquisition. Missionaries have battled hard
and with great sincerity to overcome these difficulties, but
in my experience much of what they teach natives is quite
unintelligible to those among whom they labour, and many
of them would, I think, recognize this. The solution often
adopted is to transform the minds of native children into
European minds, but then this is only in appearance a
solution. I must, having I hope brought this missionary
problem to your attention, now leave it, for these lectures are
not on missiology, a fascinating field of research, unhappily
as yet little tilled.

Nor do I therefore discuss the more general question of
translation any further here, for it cannot be treated briefly.
We all know the tag '*traduttore, traditore*'. I mention the matter
in my introductory lecture partly because we have to bear
in mind, in estimating theories of primitive religion, what
the words used in them meant to the scholars who used them.
If one is to understand the interpretations of primitive mentality they put forward, one has to know their own mentality, broadly where they stood; to enter into their way of
looking at things, a way of their class, sex, and period. As far
as religion goes, they all had, as far as I know, a religious
background in one form or another. To mention some names
which are most likely to be familiar to you: Tylor had been
brought up a Quaker, Frazer a Presbyterian, Marett in the
Church of England, Malinowski a Catholic, while Durkheim,
Lévy-Bruhl, and Freud had a Jewish background; but with
one or two exceptions, whatever the background may have

been, the persons whose writings have been most influential have been at the time they wrote agnostics or atheists. Primitive religion was with regard to its validity no different from any other religious faith, an illusion. It was not just that they asked, as Bergson put it, how it is that 'beliefs and practices which are anything but reasonable could have been, and still are, accepted by reasonable beings'.[1] It was rather that implicit in their thinking were the optimistic convictions of the eighteenth-century rationalist philosophers that people are stupid and bad only because they have bad institutions, and they have bad institutions only because they are ignorant and superstitious, and they are ignorant and superstitious because they have been exploited in the name of religion by cunning and avaricious priests and the unscrupulous classes which have supported them. We should, I think, realize what was the intention of many of these scholars if we are to understand their theoretical constructions. They sought, and found, in primitive religions a weapon which could, they thought, be used with deadly effect against Christianity. If primitive religion could be explained away as an intellectual aberration, as a mirage induced by emotional stress, or by its social function, it was implied that the higher religions could be discredited and disposed of in the same way. This intention is scarcely concealed in some cases—Frazer, King, and Clodd, for example. I do not doubt their sincerity and, as I have indicated elsewhere,[2] they have my sympathy, though not my assent. However, whether they were right or wrong is beside the point, which is that the impassioned rationalism of the time has coloured their assessment of primitive religions and has given their writings, as we read them today, a flavour of smugness which one may find either irritating or risible.

Religious belief was to these anthropologists absurd, and it is so to most anthropologists of yesterday and today. But some explanation of the absurdity seemed to be required, and it was offered in psychological or sociological terms. It

---

[1] H. Bergson, *The Two Sources of Morality and Religion*, 1956 edit., p. 103.

[2] 'Religion and the Anthropologists', *Blackfriars*, Apr. 1960. Reprinted in *Essays in Social Anthropology*, 1962.

was the intention of writers on primitive religion to explain it by its origins, so the explanations would obviously account for the essential features of all and every religion, including the higher ones. Either explicitly or implicitly, explanation of the religion of primitives was made out to hold for the origins of all that was called 'early' religion and hence of the faith of Israel and, by implication, that of Christianity which arose from it. Thus, as Andrew Lang put it, 'the theorist who believes in ancestor-worship as the key of all the creeds will see in Jehovah a developed ancestral ghost, or a kind of fetish-god, attached to a stone—perhaps an ancient sepulchral stele of some desert sheikh. The exclusive admirer of the hypothesis of Totemism will find evidence for his belief in worship of the golden calf and the bulls. The partisan of nature-worship will insist on Jehovah's connection with storm, thunder, and the fire of Sinai.'[1]

We may, indeed, wonder why they did not take as their first field of study the higher religions about whose history, theology, and rites far more was known than of the religions of the primitives, thus proceeding from the better known to the less known. They may to some extent have ignored the higher religions to avoid controversy and embarrassment in the somewhat delicate circumstances then obtaining, but it was chiefly because they wanted to discover the origin of religion, the essence of it, and they thought that this would be found in very primitive societies. However some of them may have protested that by 'origin' they did not mean earliest in time but simplest in structure, the implicit assumption in their arguments was that what was simplest in structure must have been that from which more developed forms evolved. This ambiguity in the concept of origin has caused much confusion in anthropology. I say no more about it at this stage but I will revert to it, and to other general matters so far briefly touched on, in my final lecture, by which time I shall have had an opportunity to place some examples of anthropological theories of religion before you. We may, however, note here that had the authors whose writings we are going to examine read at all deeply into, shall we say,

[1] Andrew Lang, *The Making of Religion*, 1898, p. 294.

Christian theology, history, exegesis, apologetics, symbolic thought, and ritual, they would have been much better placed to assess accounts of primitive religious ideas and practices. But it was rare indeed that those scholars who set themselves up as authorities on primitive religion showed in their interpretations that they had more than a superficial understanding of the historical religions and of what the ordinary worshipper in them believes, what meaning what he does has for him, and how he feels when he does it.

What I have said does not imply that the anthropologist *has* to have a religion of his own, and I think we should be clear on this point at the outset. He is not concerned, *qua* anthropologist, with the truth or falsity of religious thought. As I understand the matter, there is no possibility of his *knowing* whether the spiritual beings of primitive religions or of any others have any existence or not, and since that is the case he cannot take the question into consideration. The beliefs are for him sociological facts, not theological facts, and his sole concern is with their relation to each other and to other social facts. His problems are scientific, not metaphysical or ontological. The method he employs is that now often called the phenomenological one—a comparative study of beliefs and rites, such as god, sacrament, and sacrifice, to determine their meaning and social significance. The validity of the belief lies in the domain of what may broadly be designated the philosophy of religion. It was precisely because so many anthropological writers did take up a theological position, albeit a negative and implicit one, that they felt that an explanation of primitive religious phenomena in causal terms was required, going, it seems to me, beyond the legitimate bounds of the subject.

Later I shall embark on a general review of anthropological theories of religion. Permit me to say that I have read the books I shall criticize, for one finds only too often that students accept what others have written about what an author wrote instead of reading the author himself (Lévy-Bruhl's books, for example, have time and again been grossly misrepresented by persons who, I am sure, have read them either not at all or not with diligence). In making this review we shall find that it will often be unnecessary for me to point out the inadequacies of one or other point of view because the required criticism is contained in the writings of other authors mentioned later. This being so, it may be well to add, and I am sure you will agree, that it must not be supposed that there can be only one sort of general statement which can be made about social phenomena, and that others must be wrong if that one is right. There is no *a priori* reason why these theories purporting to explain primitive religion in terms respectively of ratiocination, emotion, and social function should not all be correct, each supplementing the others, though I do not believe that they are. Interpretation can be on different levels. Likewise there is no reason why several different explanations of the same type, or on the same level, should not all be right so long as they do not contradict each other, for each may explain different features of the same phenomenon. In point of fact, however, I find all the theories we shall examine together no more than plausible and even, as they have been propounded, unacceptable in that they contain contradictions and other logical inadequacies, or in that they cannot, as stated, be proved either true or false, or finally, and most to the point, in that ethnographic evidence invalidates them.

A final word: some people today find it embarrassing to hear peoples described as primitives or natives, and even more so to hear them spoken of as savages. But I am sometimes obliged to use the designations of my authors, who wrote in the robust language of a time when offence to the peoples they wrote about could scarcely be given, the good time of Victorian prosperity and progress, and, one may add, smugness, our pomp of yesterday. But the words are used by me in what Weber calls a value-free sense, and they are etymologically unobjectionable. In any case, the use of the word 'primitive' to describe peoples living in small-scale societies with a simple material culture and lacking literature is too firmly established to be eliminated. This is unfortunate, because no word has caused greater confusion in anthropological writings, as you will see, for it can have a logical and a chronological sense and the two senses have sometimes not been kept distinct, even in the minds of good scholars.

So much by way of some introductory remarks, which were necessary before embarking on our voyage into an ocean of past thought. As is the case with any, and every, science we shall find on many an isle the graves of shipwrecked sailors; but when we look back on the whole history of human thought we need not despair because as yet we know so little of the nature of primitive religion, or, indeed, of religion in general, and because we have to dismiss as merely conjectural, merely plausible, theories purporting to explain it. Rather we must take courage and pursue our studies in the spirit of the dead sailor of the Greek Anthology epigram:

> A shipwrecked sailor, buried on this coast,
>   Bids you set sail.
> Full many a gallant bark, when we were lost,
>   Weathered the gale.

II

PSYCHOLOGICAL THEORIES

THE theory of President de Brosses,[1] a contemporary and correspondent of Voltaire, that religion originated in fetishism, was accepted until the middle of last century. The thesis, taken up by Comte,[2] was that fetishism, the worship, according to Portuguese sailors, of inanimate things and of animals by the coastal Negroes of West Africa, developed into polytheism and polytheism into monotheism. It was replaced by theories, couched in intellectualist terms and under the influence of the associationalist psychology of the time, which may be designated as the ghost theory and the soul theory, both taking it for granted that primitive man is essentially rational, though his attempts to explain puzzling phenomena are crude and fallacious.

But before these theories became generally accepted they had to contest the field with others of the nature-myth school, a contest all the more bitterly fought in that both were of the same intellectualist genre. I discuss very briefly the nature myth account of the origin of religion first, partly because it was first in time, and also because what happened later was a reaction to animistic theories, nature mythology having ceased, at any rate in this country, to have any following and significance.

The nature-myth school was predominantly a German school, and it was mostly concerned with Indo-European religions, its thesis being that the gods of antiquity, and by implication gods anywhere and at all times, were no more than personified natural phenomena: sun, moon, stars, dawn, the spring renewal, mighty rivers, &c. The most powerful representative of this school was Max Müller (son

---

[1] Ch. R. de Brosses, *Du Culte des dieux fétiches ou parallèle de l'ancienne religion de l'Egypte avec la religion actuelle de la Nigritie*, 1760.
[2] Comte, *Cours de philosophie positive*, 1908 edit., 52e–54e leçon.

of the romantic poet Wilhelm Müller), a German scholar of
the solar-myth branch of the school (the various branches did
a good deal of wrangling among themselves), who spent most
of his life at Oxford, where he was Professor and a Fellow of
All Souls. He was a linguist of quite exceptional ability, one
of the leading Sanskritists of his time, and in general a man of
great erudition; and he has been most unjustly decried. He
was not prepared to go as far as some of his more extreme
German colleagues, not just because at Oxford in those days
it was dangerous to be an agnostic, but from conviction, for
he was a pious and sentimental Lutheran; but he got fairly
near their position, and, by tacking and veering in his many
books to avoid it, he rendered his thought sometimes ambiguous and opaque. In his view, as I understand it, men have
always had an intuition of the divine, the idea of the Infinite—his word for God—deriving from sensory experiences;
so we do not have to seek its source in primitive revelation or
in a religious instinct or faculty, as some people then did.
All human knowledge comes through the senses, that of
touch giving the sharpest impression of reality, and all
reasoning is based on them, and this is true of religion also:
nihil in fide quod non ante fuerit in sensu. Now, things which are
intangible, like the sun and the sky, gave men the idea of the
infinite and also furnished the material for deities. Max
Müller did not wish to be understood as suggesting that
religion began by men deifying grand natural objects, but
rather that these gave him a feeling of the infinite and also
served as symbols for it.

Müller was chiefly interested in the gods of India and of the
classical world, though he tried his hand at the interpretation of some primitive material and certainly believed that
his explanations had general validity. His thesis was that the
infinite, once the idea had arisen, could only be thought of in
metaphor and symbol, which could only be taken from what
seemed majestic in the known world, such as the heavenly
bodies, or rather their attributes. But these attributes then
lost their original metaphorical sense and achieved autonomy
by becoming personified as deities in their own right. The
nomina became *numina*. So religions, of this sort at any rate,

might be described as a 'disease of language', a pithy but unfortunate expression which later Müller tried to explain away but never quite lived down. It follows, he held, that the only way we can discover the meaning of the religion of early man is by philological and etymological research, which restores to the names of gods and the stories told about them their original sense. Thus, Apollo loved Daphne; Daphne fled before him and was changed into a laurel tree. This legend makes no sense till we know that originally Apollo was a solar deity, and Daphne, the Greek name for the laurel, or rather the bay tree, was the name for the dawn. This tells us the original meaning of the myth: the sun chasing away the dawn.

Müller deals with belief in the human soul and its ghostly form in a similar manner. When men wished to express a distinction between the body and something they felt in them other than the body, the name that suggested itself was breath, something immaterial and obviously connected with life. Then this word 'psyche' came to express the principle of life, and then the soul, the mind, the self. After death the psyche went into Hades, the place of the invisible. Once the opposition of body to soul had thus been established in language and thought, philosophy began its work on it, and spiritualistic and materialistic systems of philosophy arose; and all this to put together again what language had severed. So language exercises a tyranny over thought, and thought is always struggling against it, but in vain. Similarly, the word for ghost originally meant breath, and the word for shades (of the departed) meant shadows. They were at first figurative expressions which eventually achieved concreteness.

There can be no doubt that Müller and his fellow nature mythologists carried their theories to the point of absurdity; he claimed that the siege of Troy was no more than a solar myth: and to reduce this sort of interpretation to farce, someone, I believe, wrote a pamphlet inquiring whether Max Müller himself was not a solar myth! Leaving out of consideration the mistakes in classical scholarship we now known to have been such, it is evident that, however ingenious explanations of the kind might be, they were not, and could not be, supported by adequate historical evidence to carry conviction, and could only be, at best, erudite guesswork. I need not recall the charges brought against the nature mythologists by their contemporaries, because although Max Müller, their chief representative, for a time had some influence on anthropological thought, it did not last, and Müller outlived such influence as he had once had. Spencer and Tylor, the latter strongly supported in this matter by his pupil Andrew Lang, were hostile to nature-myth theories, and their advocacy of a different approach proved successful.

Herbert Spencer, from whom anthropology has taken some of its most important methodological concepts and whom it has forgotten, devotes a large part of his *The Principles of Sociology*[1] to a discussion of primitive beliefs, and though his interpretation of them is similar to that of Sir Edward Tylor and was published after Tylor's *Primitive Culture*, his views were formulated long before his book appeared, and were independently reached. Primitive man, he says, is rational, and, given his small knowledge, his inferences are reasonable, if weak. He sees that such phenomena as sun and moon, clouds and stars, come and go, and this gives him the notion of duality, of visible and invisible conditions, and this notion is strengthened by other observations, for example, of fossils, chick and egg, chrysalis and butterfly, for Spencer had got it into his head that rude peoples have no idea of natural explanation, as though they could have conducted their various practical pursuits without it! And if other things could be dualities, why not man himself? His shadow and his reflection in water also come and go. But it is dreams, which are real experiences to primitive peoples, which chiefly gave man the idea of his own duality, and he identified the dream-self which wanders at night with the shadow-self which appears by day. This idea of duality is fortified by experiences of various forms of temporary insensibility, sleeping, swooning, catalepsy, and the like, so that death itself comes to be thought of as only a prolonged form of insensibility. And if man has a double,

[1] Spencer, op. cit., vol. i.

a soul, by the same reasoning so must animals have one and also plants and material objects.

The origin of religion, however, is to be looked for in the belief in ghosts rather than in souls. That the soul has a temporary after-life is suggested by the appearance of the dead in dreams, so long as the dead are remembered; and the first traceable conception of a supernatural being is that of a ghost. This conception must be earlier than that of fetish, which implies the existence of an indwelling ghost or spirit. Also, the idea of ghosts is found everywhere, unlike that of fetishes, which is indeed not characteristic of very primitive peoples. The idea of ghosts inevitably—Spencer's favourite word—develops into that of gods, the ghosts of remote ancestors or of superior persons becoming divinities (the doctrine of Euhemerism), and the food and drink placed on their graves to please the dead becoming sacrifices and libations to the gods to propitiate them. So he concludes that 'ancestor-worship is the root of every religion'.[1]

All this is served up in inappropriate terms borrowed from the physical sciences and in a decidedly didactic manner. The argument is *a priori* speculation, sprinkled with some illustrations, and is specious. It is a fine example of the introspectionist psychologist's, or 'if I were a horse', fallacy, to which I shall have to make frequent reference. If Spencer were living in primitive conditions, those would, he assumed, have been the steps by which he would have reached the beliefs which primitives hold. It does not seem to have occurred to him to ask himself how, if the ideas of soul and ghost arose from such fallacious reasoning about clouds and butterflies and dreams and trances, the beliefs could have persisted throughout millennia and could still be held by millions of civilized people in his day and ours.

Tylor's theory (for which he owed a debt to Comte) of animism—he coined the word—is very similar to that of Spencer, though, as the word *anima* implies, he stresses the idea of soul rather than of ghost. Some ambiguity attaches to the term 'animism' in anthropological writings, it being sometimes employed in the sense of the belief, ascribed to

[1] Op. cit. i. 440.

primitive peoples, that not only creatures but also inanimate objects have life and personality, and sometimes with the further sense that in addition they have souls. Tylor's theory covers both senses, but we are particularly interested here in the second sense of the term. With regard to that, the theory consists of two main theses, the first accounting for its origin, and the second for its development. Primitive man's reflections on such experiences as death, disease, trances, visions, and above all dreams, led him to the conclusion that they are to be accounted for by the presence or absence of some immaterial entity, the soul. Both the ghost theory and the soul theory might be regarded as two versions of a dream theory of the origin of religion. Primitive man then transferred this idea of soul to other creatures in some ways like himself, and even to inanimate objects which aroused his interest. The soul, being detachable from whatever it lodged in, could be thought of as independent of its material home, whence arose the idea of spiritual beings, whose supposed existence constituted Tylor's minimum definition of religion; and these finally developed into gods, beings vastly superior to man and in control of his destiny.

The objections already made to Spencer's theory hold also for Tylor's. In the absence of any possible means of knowing how the idea of soul and spirit originated and how they might have developed, a logical construction of the scholar's mind is posited on primitive man, and put forward as the explanation of his beliefs. The theory has the quality of a just-so story like 'how the leopard got his spots'. The ideas of soul and spirit could have arisen in the way Tylor supposed, but there is no evidence that they did. At best it might be shown that primitives cite dreams as evidence for the existence of souls and souls for the existence of spirits, but even if that could be done, it would not prove that dreams gave birth to the one idea or souls to the other. Swanton rightly protests against such causal explanations, asking why, when a man dies and someone dreams of him afterwards, it is an 'obvious inference' (Tylor) that he has a phantom life divisible from the body. Obvious to whom? The same author also points out that there is no identity of attitude either towards the dead or to dreams among primitive peoples, and that the differences need to be accounted for if 'obvious inference' is to be accepted as a valid causal conclusion.[1]

That the idea of soul led to that of spirit is a very dubious supposition. Both ideas are present among what were called the lowest savages, who in evolutionary perspective were held to be the nearest one could get to prehistoric man; and the two conceptions are not only different but opposed, spirit being regarded as incorporeal, extraneous to man, and invasive. Indeed, Tylor, through failure to recognize a fundamental distinction between the two conceptions, made a serious blunder in his representation of early Hebraic thought, as Dr. Snaith has pointed out.[2] Also, it remains to be proved that the most primitive peoples think that creatures and material objects have souls like their own. If any peoples can be said to be dominantly animistic, in Tylor's sense of the word, they belong to much more advanced cultures, a fact which, though it would have no historical significance for me, would be highly damaging to the evolutionary argument; as is also the fact that the conception of a god is found among all the so-called lowest hunters and collectors. Finally, we may ask again how it is that, if religion is the product of so elementary an illusion, it has displayed so great a continuity and persistence.

Tylor wished to show that primitive religion was rational, that it arose from observations, however inadequate, and from logical deductions from them, however faulty; that it constituted a crude natural philosophy. In his treatment of magic, which he distinguished from religion rather for convenience of exposition than on grounds of aetiology or validity, he likewise stressed the rational element in what he called 'this farrago of nonsense'. It also is based on genuine observation, and rests further on classification of similarities, the first essential process in human knowledge. Where the magician goes wrong is in inferring that because things are alike they have a mystical link between them, thus mistaking

[1] J. R. Swanton, 'Three Factors in Primitive Religion', *American Anthropologist*, n.s. xxvi (1924), 358–65.
[2] N. H. Snaith, *The Distinctive Ideas of the Old Testament*, 1944, p. 148.

an ideal connexion for a real one, a subjective one for an objective one. And if we ask how peoples who exploit nature and organize their social life so well make such mistakes, the answer is that they have very good reasons for not perceiving the futility of their magic. Nature, or trickery on the part of the magician, often brings about what the magic is supposed to achieve; and if it fails to achieve its purpose, that is rationally explained by neglect of some prescription, or by the fact that some prohibition has been ignored or some hostile force has impeded it. Also, there is plasticity about judgements of success and failure, and people everywhere find it hard to appreciate evidence, especially when the weight of authority induces acceptance of what confirms, and rejection of what contradicts, a belief. Here Tylor's observations are borne out by ethnological evidence.

I have touched briefly on Tylor's discussions of magic partly as a further illustration of intellectualist interpretation and partly because it leads me straight to an estimation of Sir James Frazer's contribution to our subject. Frazer is, I suppose, the best-known name in anthropology, and we owe much to him and to Spencer and Tylor. The whole of *The Golden Bough*, a work of immense industry and erudition, is devoted to primitive superstitions. But it cannot be said that he added much of value to Tylor's theory of religion; rather that he introduced some confusion into it in the form of two new suppositions, the one pseudo-historical and the other psychological. According to him, mankind everywhere, and sooner or later, passes through three stages of intellectual development, from magic to religion, and from religion to science, a scheme he may have taken over from Comte's phases, the theological, the metaphysical, and the positive, though the correspondence is far from an exact one. Other writers of the period, for example, King, Jevons, and Lubbock, and, as we shall see, in a certain way of viewing the matter, Marett, Preuss, and the writers of the *Année Sociologique* school as well, also believed that magic preceded religion. Eventually, says Frazer, the shrewder intelligences probably discovered that magic did not really achieve its ends, but, still being unable to overcome their difficulties by empirical means and to face their crises through a refined philosophy, they fell into another illusion, that there were spiritual beings who could aid them. In course of time the shrewder intelligences saw that spirits were equally bogus, an enlightenment which heralded the dawn of experimental science. The arguments in support of this thesis were, to say the least, trivial, and it was ethnologically most vulnerable. In particular, the conclusions based on Australian data were wide of the mark, and, since the Australians were introduced into the argument to show that the simpler the culture, the more the magic and the less the religion, it is pertinent to note that hunting and collecting peoples, including many Australian tribes, have animistic and theistic beliefs and cults. It is also evident that the variety, and therefore volume, of magic in their cultures is likely to be less, as indeed it is, than in cultures technologically more advanced: there cannot, for instance, be agricultural magic or magic of iron-working in the absence of cultivated plants and of metals. No one accepts Frazer's theory of stages today.

The psychological part of his thesis was to oppose magic and science to religion, the first two postulating a world subject to invariable natural laws, an idea he shared with Jevons,[1] and the last a world in which events depend on the caprice of spirits. Consequently, while the magician and the scientist, strange bedfellows, perform their operations with quiet confidence, the priest performs his in fear and trembling. So psychologically science and magic are alike, though one happens to be false and the other true. This analogy between science and magic holds only in so far as both are techniques, and few anthropologists have regarded it as other than superficial. Frazer here made the same mistake in method as Lévy-Bruhl was to make, in comparing modern science with primitive magic instead of comparing empirical and magical techniques in the same cultural conditions.

However, not all that Frazer wrote about magic and religion was chaff. There was some grain. For example, he was able in his painstaking way to demonstrate what Condorcet and others had merely asserted, how frequently among the

[1] F. B. Jevons, 'Report on Greek Mythology', *Folk-Lore*, ii. 2 (1891), 220 ff.

simpler peoples of the world rulers are magicians and priests. Then, although he added little to Tylor's explanation of magic as misapplication of association of ideas, he provided some useful classificatory terms, showing that these associations are of two types, those of similarity and those of contact, homoeopathic or imitative magic and contagious magic. He did not, however, go further than to show that in magical beliefs and rites we can discern certain elementary sensations. Neither Tylor nor Frazer explained why people in their magic mistake, as they supposed, ideal connexions for real ones when they do not do so in their other activities. Moreover, it is not correct that they do so. The error here was in not recognizing that the associations are social and not psychological stereotypes, and that they occur therefore only when evoked in specific ritual situations, which are also of limited duration, as I have argued elsewhere.[1]

About all these broadly speaking intellectualist theories we must say that, if they cannot be refuted, they also cannot be sustained, and for the simple reason that there is no evidence about how religious beliefs originated. The evolutionary stages their sponsors attempted to construct, as a means of supplying the missing evidence, may have had logical consistency, but they had no historical value. However, if we must discard the evolutionist (or rather progressionist) assumptions and judgements, or give them the status of rather vague hypotheses, we may still retain much of what was claimed about the essential rationality of primitive peoples. They may not have reached their beliefs in the manner these writers supposed, but even if they did not, the element of rationality is still always there, in spite of observations being inadequate, inferences faulty, and conclusions wrong. The beliefs are always coherent, and up to a point they can be critical and sceptical, and even experimental, within the system of their beliefs and in its idiom; and their thought is therefore intelligible to anyone who cares to learn their language and study their way of life.

The animistic theory in various forms remained for many

[1] 'The Intellectualist (English) Interpretation of Magic', *Bulletin of the Faculty of Arts*, Egyptian University (Cairo), i, pt. 2 (1933), 282–311.

years unchallenged, and it left its mark on all the anthropological literature of the day, as, to give a single example,
in Dorman's comprehensive account of the religion of the
American Indians, where every belief—totemism, sorcery,
fetishism—is explained in animistic terms. But voices began
to be raised in protest, both with regard to the origin of
religion and to the order of its development.

Before we consider what they had to say, it should be
remarked that the critics had two advantages their predecessors lacked. Associationist psychology, which was more or
less a mechanistic theory of sensation, was giving way to experimental psychology, under the influence of which anthropologists were able, though in a rather common-sense way
and in their everyday meanings, to make use of its terms,
and we then hear less of the cognitive and more of the affective and conative functions, the orective elements, of the
mind; of instincts, emotions, sentiments, and later, under the
influence of psycho-analysis, of complexes, inhibitions, projection, &c.; and *Gestalt* psychology and the psychology of
crowds were also to leave their mark. But what was more
important was the great advance in ethnography in the last
decades of the nineteenth century and early in the present
century. This provided the later writers with an abundance
of information and of better quality: such researches as those
of Fison, Howitt, and Spencer and Gillen for the Australian
aboriginals; Tregear for the Maoris; Codrington, Haddon, and
Seligman for the Melanesians; Nieuwenhuis, Kruijt, Wilken,
Snouck Hurgronje, and Skeat and Blagden for the peoples of
Indonesia; Man for the Andaman Islanders; Im Thurn and
von den Steinen for the Amerindians; Boas for the Eskimoes;
and in Africa Macdonald, Kidd, Mary Kingsley, Junod,
Ellis, Dennet, and others.

It will have been noted that in one respect Frazer differed
radically from Tylor, in his claim that religion was preceded
by a magical phase. Other writers took the same view. An
American, John H. King, published in 1892 two volumes
entitled *The Supernatural: its Origin, Nature, and Evolution.*
They made little impression in the climate of animism then
prevailing, and had fallen into oblivion till resuscitated by

Wilhelm Schmidt. As intellectualist and evolutionist as others of the time, he was of the opinion that the ideas of ghost and spirit are too sophisticated for rude men, a view which follows logically from the basic assumption of the evolutionary thought of the time, that everything develops from something simpler and cruder. There must, he thought, be an earlier stage than animism, a *mana* stage in which the idea of luck, of the canny and uncanny, was the sole constituent of what he called the supernal. This arose from faulty deductions from observations of physical states and organic processes, leading primitive man to suppose that the virtue, the *mana*, was in objects and events themselves as an intrinsic property of them. Hence arose the doctrine of spells and charms, and the stage of magic came into being. Then, through errors of judgement and faulty reasoning about dreams and acquired neurotic states, arose the idea of ghosts, and finally, by a succession of steps, that of spirits and gods, the various stages depending upon a general development of social institutions. So religion was for King also an illusion. Furthermore, it was a disaster which stayed intellectual and moral progress; and primitive peoples who believe such fables are like small children, ontogenic development here corresponding to phylogenic (what psychologists used to call the doctrine of recapitulation).

That there must have been an earlier and cruder stage of religion than the animistic one was asserted by other writers besides Frazer and King, Preuss in Germany and Marett in this country being two of the best known of them, and they presented a challenge to Tylor's theory which had for so many years held the field; but in some cases the challenge was concerned only with the question of time and order of development, and the critics in this matter failed to prove that there has ever been such a stage of thought as they postulated. The most radical and damaging attack came from two of Tylor's pupils, Andrew Lang and R. R. Marett.

Like his contemporaries, Andrew Lang was an evolutionary theorist, but he refused to accept that gods could have developed out of ghosts or spirits. He wrote with much good sense—though with some nonsense also—but, partly because the animistic origin of religion was so generally taken as evident, what he said about primitive religion was ignored till he was later vindicated by Wilhelm Schmidt. It was also because he was a romantic man of letters who wrote on such subjects as Prince Charles Edward and Mary Stuart, and so could be dismissed as a littérateur and dilettante. He was an animist in that he agreed with Tylor that belief in souls, and subsequently in spirits, might well have arisen from psychical phenomena (dreams, &c.), but he was not prepared to accept that the idea of God arose as a late development from the notions of souls, ghosts, and spirits. He pointed out that the conception of a creative, moral, fatherly, omnipotent, and omniscient God is found among the most primitive peoples of the globe, and is probably to be accounted for by what used to be known as the argument from design, a rational conclusion by primitive man that the world around him must have been made by some superior being. However this might be, on the evolutionists' own criteria, the idea of God, being found among the culturally simplest peoples, could not be a late development from the ideas of ghost and soul or indeed anything else. Moreover, says Lang, the supreme being of these peoples is, at any rate in many cases, not thought of as spirit at all, at least in our sense of divine spirit—'God is a spirit, and they who worship him must worship him in spirit and in truth'—but rather as what we might speak of as some sort of person. Therefore he concludes that the conception of God 'need not be evolved out of reflections on dreams and "ghosts"'.[1] The soul-ghost and God have totally different sources, and monotheism may even have preceded animism, though the point of priority can never be historically settled; but in spite of this sensible assessment, Lang clearly thought that monotheism was prior, and was corrupted and degraded by later animistic ideas. The two streams of religious thought finally came together, the one through Hebrew and the other through Hellenistic sources, in Christianity.

Very different was Marett's line of argument. He not only advocated a pre-animistic stage but challenged on methodological grounds the whole line of reasoning behind the

[1] Lang, *The Making of Religion*, p. 2.

explanation of religion that had been put forward. Primitive man, he claimed, was not at all like the philosopher *manqué* he had been made out to be. With early man it is not ideas which give rise to action, but action which gives rise to ideas: 'savage religion is something not so much thought out as danced out.'[1] It is the motor side to primitive religion which is significant, not its reflective side, and the action derives from affective states. Marett drew the conclusion that therefore in the earliest, the pre-animistic, stage, religion cannot be differentiated from magic, as it can be at a later stage when magic is condemned by organized religion and acquires a dyslogistic sense. He thought it better, when speaking of primitive peoples, to use the expression 'magico-religious', a usage, and in my opinion an unfortunate one, adopted by a number of anthropologists, among them Rivers and Seligman. However, Marett himself preferred to speak of both as *mana*, a Melanesian word anthropologists had adopted into their conceptual vocabulary with, I believe, disastrous results, for, though we cannot discuss so complicated a matter now, it seems clear that *mana* did not mean to those to whose languages the word belonged the impersonal force —an almost metaphysical conception—which Marett and others, for example, King, Preuss, Durkheim, and Hubert and Mauss, following the information they then had, thought it did. According to Marett, primitive peoples have a feeling that there is an occult power in certain persons and things, and it is the presence or absence of this feeling which cuts off the sacred from the profane, the wonderworld from the workaday world, it being the function of taboos to separate the one world from the other; and this feeling is the emotion of awe, a compound of fear, wonder, admiration, interest, respect, perhaps even love. Whatever evokes this emotion and is treated as a mystery is religion. Why some things should evoke this response and not others, and why among some peoples and not among others, Marett does not tell us: indeed, his illustrative examples are sparse, and thrown into the argument quite haphazardly.

Though he says that magic cannot at this stage be differ-

[1] R. R. Marett, *The Threshold of Religion*, 2nd edit. (1914), p. xxxi.

entiated from religion, he nevertheless offers a different explanation of magic, though of the same emotionalist order. Magic arises out of emotional tension. A man is overcome by hate or love or some other emotion, and, since there is nothing practical he can do about it, he resorts to make-believe to relieve the tension, as a man might throw into the fire the portrait of his faithless mistress. This is what Marett calls rudimentary magic (Vierkandt reasons in the same way). When such situations are sufficiently recurrent, the response becomes stabilized as what he calls developed magic, a socially recognized mode of customary behaviour. Then the magician is well aware of the difference between symbol and realization. He knows that he is not doing the real thing, that pointing a spear at an enemy at a distance while reciting incantations against him is not the same as throwing a spear at him at close range. He does not, as Tylor made out, mistake an ideal connexion for a real one; and hence also there is no true analogy, as Frazer held, between magic and science, for the savage is well aware of the difference between magical and mechanical causation, between symbolic and empirical action. So magic is a substitute activity in situations in which practical means to attain an end are lacking, and its function is either cathartic or stimulating, giving men courage, relief, hope, tenacity. In his article on magic in Hasting's *Encyclopaedia of Religion and Ethics* Marett gives a somewhat different, though also a cathartic, explanation of certain forms of magical expression.[1] Recurrent situations in the social life generate states of emotional intensity which, if they cannot find a vent in activity directed to a practical end, such as hunting, fighting, and love-making, have to be exhausted in secondary, or substitute, activity, such as dances which play at hunting, fighting, and love-making; but here the function of the substitute activity is to serve as an outlet for superfluous energy. Then these substitute activities change from being surrogates to become auxiliaries to empirical action, retaining their mimetic form, though in reality they are repercussions rather than imitations.

As compared with his contribution towards an under-

[1] Marett, Hasting's *Encyclopaedia of Religion and Ethics*, 1915, vol. viii.

standing of magic, Marett had little of positive significance to say about primitive religion. There was, indeed, much talk about the 'sacred', in which, I suspect, he owed a good deal to Durkheim, but it amounted to little more than juggling with words. Maybe he found himself, as a Fellow of an Oxford college at that time, in an equivocal position; and, being a philosopher, he was able to (appear to) get out of it by distinguishing between the task of social anthropology to determine the origin of religion—a mixture of history and causation—and the task of theology, which was concerned with its validity;[1] a position we all to some extent take up. His conclusion is that 'The end and result of primitive religion is, in a word, the consecration of life, the stimulation of the will to live and to do'.[2]

Marett was a brilliant writer, but this genial and ebullient classical philosopher, who by a single short paper established himself as the leader of the pre-animistic school, did not set forth the weight of evidence required to support his theories, and neither his influence nor his reputation lasted long. Nor was it enough, though what he said was amusing and there is an element of truth in it, to say (in conversation) that to understand primitive mentality there was no need to go and live among savages, the experience of an Oxford Common Room being sufficient.

I speak very briefly of the writings, which were prolific, of another classical scholar, a school headmaster, Ernest Crawley, whose books were appearing at much the same time as Marett's. He exercised much good sense in knocking down some erroneous theories still current at the time, such as those of group marriage, primitive communism, and marriage by capture, but his positive contributions were less valuable. In discussing religion in *The Idea of the Soul* he followed Tylor in supposing that the conception of spirit arose from that of soul and in a later stage of culture became that of God, but he disagreed with him about the genesis of the idea of soul.

---

[1] Marett, 'Origin and Validity in Religion' (first pub. in 1916) and 'Magic or Religion?' (first pub. in 1919), *Psychology and Folk-Lore* (1920). Cf. also article cited in next note.
[2] 'Religion (Primitive Religion)', *Ency. Brit.*, 11th edit., xix. 105.

Tylor's view on this question, so Crawley said, took us no further than Hobbes or Aristotle, and it is psychologically impossible for the idea of soul to have originated from dreams, &c. Rather, it arose from sensation. Primitive man could visualize any person he knew when that person was absent, and from this duality arose the ideas of soul and ghost; and it follows that everything of which a mental image can be formed can have a soul, though the souls of inanimate objects are not thought, any more than the objects themselves, to be animated, as Tylor believed. So 'Spiritual existence is mental existence; the world of spirits is the mental world'.[1] As for God or gods, they are no more than aggregates of ghosts or ghosts of prominent individuals, which is what Spencer had said. Religion is thus an illusion.

If this were all Crawley wrote about religion, he could have been placed in the intellectualist class, and what general comments have been made about that class would apply to him also. But in other of his writings, including his earlier and best-known work *The Mystic Rose*, which I, like some of his contemporaries, find rather unintelligible, he appears to have a more general theory of religion. Primitive man's whole mental habit is religious or superstitious, and magic is therefore not to be distinguished from religion. In his ignorance he lives in a world of mystery in which he does not distinguish between subjective and objective reality; and the drive behind all his thought is fear, especially of the danger in social relations, and particularly those between men and women. This feeling is partly instinctive and partly due to a more or less subconscious idea that properties and qualities, being infectious, can be transmitted through contact. Therefore men feel themselves to be particularly vulnerable when engaged in physiological actions such as eating and sexual congress, and that is why these actions are hedged round with taboos. He concludes that 'All living religious conceptions spring from more or less constant functional origins, physiological and psychological'.[2] He even speaks of 'physiological thought',[3] the process of functions producing, by a more

---

[1] A. E. Crawley, *The Idea of the Soul*, 1909, p. 78.
[2] Crawley, *The Mystic Rose*, 1927 edit., i. 86.   [3] Ibid. 215.

or less organic reflex, ideas concerning them. In this theory primitive religion amounts practically to taboo, the product of fear; the spirits in which primitive peoples believe being no more than conceptualizations of danger and fear. I find it difficult to reconcile this position with the statement in *The Idea of the Soul* that the soul is 'the basis of all religion'[1] but, as I have said, I do not find Crawley a very lucid writer. His general theme, however, is the same in all his books: religion is ultimately only a product of primitive man's fear, diffidence, lack of initiative, and of his ignorance and inexperience; and it is not a thing in itself, a department of social life, but rather a tone or spirit which permeates every part of it and is chiefly concerned with the fundamental processes of organic life and climacteric events. The vital instinct, the will to live, is identical with religious feeling. Religion makes sacred what promotes life, health, and strength. When we ask what the religious emotion is, we are told that it is nothing specific, 'but that tone or quality of any feeling which results in making something sacred'.[2] It follows from Crawley's argument, as he himself says, that the greater the dangers, the more the religion, and therefore the more primitive stages of culture are more religious than the later ones, and women are more religious than men; and also, that God is a product of psycho-biological processes.

Before commenting on Marett's and Crawley's explanations of religion and magic, let us consider a few further similar examples.

I suppose a few words should be said here about Wilhelm Wundt, an influential figure of the time, though now seldom referred to. An eclectic writer, he is not easy to place. His *Völkerpsychologie* approach undoubtedly influenced Durkheim, but in the main it can be said that his explanations were psychological, as well as being highly evolutionary, and also speculative and somewhat tedious. Ideas which refer to what is not directly amenable to perception, mythological thinking as he calls it, originate in emotional processes (chiefly fear—*Scheu*), 'which are projected outward into the

---

[1] Crawley, *The Idea of the Soul*, 1909, p. 1.
[2] Id., *The Tree of Life*, 1905, p. 209.

environment'.[1] First comes belief in magic and demons, and it is not till the next evolutionary stage, the Totemic Age, that we have the beginnings of religion proper in the worship of animals. Then, as totemism fades, the totem-ancestor of the clan is replaced by the human ancestor as the object of worship. Ancestor worship then issues in hero cult, and then in the cult of the gods—the Age of Heroes and Gods. The final stage is the Humanistic Age with its religious universalism. Perhaps all this should be labelled philosophy of history rather than as anthropology. Certainly it reads very oddly to the anthropologist of today.

We have now reached the era of field-working anthropologists, who had studied native peoples at first hand, and not in accounts written by other, and untrained, observers. R. H. Lowie, whose study of the Crow Indians was an important contribution to anthropology, tells us that primitive religion is characterized by 'a sense of the Extraordinary, Mysterious, or Supernatural'[2] (note the capital letters), and the religious response is that of 'amazement and awe; and its source is in the Supernatural, Extraordinary, Weird, Sacred, Holy, Divine'[3] (again, note the capital letters). Like Crawley, he held that there is no specifically religious behaviour, only religious feelings, so the belief of the Crow Indians in the existence of ghosts of the dead is not religious belief, because the subject is of no emotional interest to them; and so the militant atheist and the priest can both be religious persons, if they experience the same feelings, and Christian dogma and the theory of biological evolution may both be religious doctrines. Positivism, egalitarianism, absolutism, and the cult of reason are all likewise indistinguishable from religion; and one's country's flag is a typical religious symbol. When magic is associated with emotion, it also is religion. Otherwise it is psychologically equivalent to our science, as Frazer said.

Paul Radin, another American, whose study of the Winnebago Indians was also noteworthy, took up much the same

[1] W. Wundt, *Elements of Folk Psychology*, 1916, p. 74.
[2] R. H. Lowie, *Primitive Religion*, 1925, p. xvi.
[3] Ibid., p. 322.

position. There is no specific religious behaviour, only a religious feeling, a more than normal sensitiveness to certain beliefs and customs, 'which manifests itself in a thrill, a feeling of exhilaration, exaltation and awe and in a complete absorption in internal sensations'.[1] Almost any belief can become associated with this religious feeling, though it is particularly associated with values of success, happiness, and long life (one catches the echo of William James's 'religion of healthy-mindedness'); and the religious thrill is particularly evident in the crises of life, such as puberty and death. When what is generally regarded as magic arouses the religious emotion, it is religion. Otherwise it is folklore.

To cite a final American anthropologist, and a brilliant one, Goldenweiser: he also says that the two realms of the supernatural, magic and religion, are both characterized by the 'religious thrill'.[2]

As a field worker, Malinowski has put anthropologists for all time in his debt, but in his explicitly theoretical writings he displayed little originality or distinction of thought. Differentiating, as others did, between the sacred and the profane, he claimed that what distinguished the sacred was that its acts were carried out with reverence and awe. Where magic differs from religion is that religious rites have no ulterior purpose, the objective being attained in the rites themselves, as in natal, puberty, and mortuary ceremonies, whereas in magic the end is indeed believed to be attained by the rites, but not in them, as in ritual for cultivating or fishing. Psychologically, however, they are alike, for the function of both is cathartic. Faced with life's crises, and especially that of death, men in their fear and anxiety release their tensions and overcome their despair by the performance of religious rites. Malinowski's discussion of magic in his later writings[3] follows so closely part of Marett's

[1] P. Radin, *Social Anthropology*, 1932, p. 244.
[2] Goldenweiser, *Early Civilization*, 1921, p. 346.
[3] Malinowski, 'Magic, Science and Religion', *Science, Religion and Reality*, 1925. In an earlier essay, 'The Economic Aspect of the Intichiuma Ceremonies', *Festskrift Tillëgnad Edvard Westermarck*, 1912, he was more interested in the part played by magic, the magical element in totemism in particular, in economic evolution.

thesis that little need be said about it. Like religion, it arises and functions in situations of emotional stress. Men have inadequate knowledge to overcome by empirical means difficulties in their pursuits, so they use magic as a substitute activity, and this releases the tension set up between impotence and desire which threatens the success of their enterprises. Hence the mimetic form of the rites, the enactment of acts suggested by the desired ends. So magic produces the same subjective result as empirical action would have done, and confidence is restored, and whatever pursuit it may be that people are engaged in may be continued. This explanation is followed, without critical comment, by others, Driberg[1] and Firth,[2] for example; in fact emotionalist explanations of the kind were common among writers on the subject at this period. Even as well-balanced a student of primitive life as R. Thurnwald would account for primitive peoples' mistaking an ideal connexion for a real one—the Tylor–Frazer formula —by saying that their magical actions are so charged with emotion, their desires being so strong, that they inhibit the more practical modes of thought that dominate other departments of their lives.[3] Perhaps the best statement of this point of view—that magic is a product of emotional states, of desire, fear, hate, and so forth, and that its function is to relieve men of anxiety and give them hope and confidence—was that by a psychologist, Carveth Read, in a book which seems to have almost completely escaped the attention of anthropologists, *The Origin of Man and of his Superstitions*,[4] in which he discusses magic and animism under the heading of 'imagination-beliefs' as contrasted with 'perception-beliefs', those of common sense and science, which are derived from and controlled by sensory perception.

It is necessary to say something, albeit little, about Freud's contribution. A convenient bridge into his thought is provided by, among others, Van Der Leeuw. Primitive peoples, he says, do not perceive the contradictions which underlie much

---

[1] J. H. Driberg, *At Home with the Savage*, n.d. (1932), pp. 188 ff.
[2] R. Firth, 'Magic. Primitive', *Ency. Brit.*, 1955 edit., p. xiv.
[3] R. Thurnwald, 'Zauber, Allgemein', *Reallexikon der Vorgeschichte*, 1929.
[4] C. Read, *The Origin of Man and of his Superstitions*, 1920, *passim*.

of their thought because 'an imperious affective need prevents them from seeing the truth'.[1] They only see what they want to see, and this is especially the case with magic. When confronted with an impasse, man has the choice between overcoming it by his own ingenuity, and withdrawing into himself and overcoming it in fantasy: he can turn outwards or inwards, and inwards is the method of magic, or, to use the psychological term, *autisme*. Magicians believe that by words, spells, they can alter the world, and so they belong to that noble category of people who place an over-emphasis on thought: children, women, poets, artists, lovers, mystics, criminals, dreamers, and madmen. All attempt to deal with reality by the same psychological mechanism.

This over-emphasis on thought, the conviction that the hard wall of reality can be broken through in the mind, or indeed is not there at all, was what Freud claimed to have found in his neurotic patients, and called omnipotence of thought (*Allmacht der Gedanken*). The magic rites and spells of primitive man correspond psychologically to the obsessional actions and protective formulas of neurotics; so the neurotic is like the savage in that he 'believes he can change the outer world by a mere thought of his'.[2] Here again we have put before us a parallelism between ontogenic and phylogenic development: the individual passes through three libidinous phases, narcissism, object finding, which is characterized by dependence on the parents, and the state of maturity in which the individual accepts reality and adapts himself to it; and these phases correspond psychologically to the three stages in the intellectual development of man, the animistic (by which Freud seems to have meant what others would have called the magical), the religious, and the scientific. In the narcissistic phase, corresponding to magic, the child, unable to satisfy its desires through motor activity, compensates by overcoming its difficulties in imagination, substituting thought for action; he is then under analogous psychic conditions to the magician; and the neurotic is like the magician

---

[1] G. Van Der Leeuw, 'Le Structure de la mentalité primitive', *La Revue d'Histoire et de Philosophie Religieuse*, 1928, p. 14.

[2] S. Freud, *Totem and Taboo*, n.d., p. 145.

too, in that they both over-estimate the power of thought. In other words, it is tension, an acute sense of frustration, which generates magical ritual, the function of which is to relieve the tension. So magic is wish-fulfilment by which man experiences gratification through motor hallucination.

Religion is equally an illusion. It arose and is maintained by feelings of guilt. Freud tells us a just-so story which only a genius could have ventured to compose, for no evidence was, or could be, adduced in support of it, though, I suppose, it could be claimed to be psychologically, or virtually, true in the sense that a myth may be said to be true in spite of being literally and historically unacceptable. Once upon a time— the tale deserves a fairy-story opening—when men were more or less ape-like creatures, the dominant father-male of the horde kept all the females for himself.[1] His sons rose against his tyranny and monopoly, desiring to pleasure the females themselves, and they killed and ate him in a cannibalistic feast, an idea Freud gleaned from Robertson Smith. Then the sons had feelings of remorse, and instituted taboos on eating their totem, identified with the father, though they did so ceremonially from time to time, thus commemorating and renewing the guilt; and they established the further interdiction on incest which is the origin of culture, for culture derives from this renunciation. Freud's theory of religion is contained in this allegorical story, for the devoured father is also God. It may be regarded as an aetiological myth, providing a background to the drama enacted in those Viennese families of whose troubles Freud made clinical analyses which he believed to hold good in essentials for all families everywhere, since they arose out of the very nature of family structure. I need not elaborate. We all know the main features of his thesis, that, to put it crudely, children both love and hate their parents, the son, deep in his unconscious, wanting to kill the father and possess the mother (the Oedipus complex), and the daughter, deep in hers,

---

[1] An idea Freud got from J. J. Atkinson. Atkinson was first cousin to Andrew Lang, who published his essay 'Primal Law' as a supplement to his own *Social Origins*, 1903. Nothing corresponding to this Cyclopean family has been discovered.

wanting to kill the mother and be possessed by the father (the Electra complex). On the surface affection and respect win, and the confidence felt in, and the dependence felt on, the father become projected and idealized and sublimated in the father-image of God. Religion is therefore an illusion, and Freud called his book on the subject *The Future of an Illusion*;[1] but it is only an illusion objectively. Subjectively, it is not so, for it is not the product of hallucination—the father is real.

There is no limit to interpretations on these lines. I have taken a specimen from Frederick Schleiter's excellent book on primitive religion, and they are his ironical words on Tanzi's *A Text-book of Mental Diseases* which I quote:

In mellifluous cadence, balanced metaphor, and with brilliant rhetorical artifice, he sets forth the parallelism,—deep, fundamental and abiding,—between primitive religion and paranoia. . . . However, those who, either through temperamental predisposition, or more rationalistic argumentation, are disposed to find some measure of justification and dignity in the religion of primitive man, will perhaps derive some measure of consolation in the fact that Tanzi rejects the parallelism between the mental processes of primitive man and those of dementia praecox.[2]

Magic and religion are thus both reduced to psychological states: tensions, frustrations, and emotions and sentiments and complexes and delusions of one sort or another.

I have given some examples of emotionalist interpretations of religion. What now are we to make of it all? In my opinion these theories are for the most part guesswork of the, once again, 'if I were a horse' type, with this difference, that instead of 'if I were a horse I would do what horses do for one or other reason' it is now 'I would do what horses do on account of one or other feeling that horses may be supposed to have'. If we were to perform rites such as primitives do, we suppose that we would be in a state of emotional turmoil, for otherwise our reason would tell us that the rites are objectively useless. It seems to me that very little evidence is

[1] *The Future of an Illusion*, 1928.
[2] F. Schleiter, *Religion and Culture*, 1919, pp. 45–47 (on E. Tanzi, *A Text-book of Mental Diseases*, English translation, 1909).

brought forward in support of these conclusions, not even by those who not only offer them but have also had the opportunity of testing them in field research.

And here we must ask some questions. What is this awe which some of the writers I have cited say is characteristic of the sacred? Some say it is the specific religious emotion; others that there is no specific religious emotion. Either way, how does one know whether a person experiences awe or thrill or whatever it may be? How does one recognize it, and how does one measure it? Moreover, as Lowie admits and others have often pointed out, the same emotional states may be found in forms of behaviour which are quite different, and even opposed, as, for example, in the behaviour of a pacifist and of a militarist. Only chaos would result were anthropologists to classify social phenomena by emotions which are supposed to accompany them, for such emotional states, if present at all, must vary not only from individual to individual, but also in the same individual on different occasions and even at different points in the same rite. It is absurd to put priest and atheist into the same category, as Lowie does; and it would be yet more absurd to say that, when a priest is saying Mass, he is not performing a religious act unless he is in a certain emotional state; and, anyhow, who knows what his emotional state might be? If we were to classify and explain social behaviour by supposed psychological states, we would indeed get some strange results. If religion is characterized by the emotion of fear, then a man fleeing in terror from a charging buffalo might be said to be performing a religious act; and if magic is characterized by its cathartic function, then a medical practitioner who relieves a patient's anxiety, on entirely clinical grounds, might be said to be performing a magical one.

There are further considerations. A great many rites which surely almost anyone would accept as religious in character, such as sacrifices, are certainly not performed in situations in which there is any possible cause for emotional unrest or feelings of mystery and awe. They are routine, and also standardized and obligatory, rites. To speak of tensions and so forth in such cases is as meaningless as to speak of them in explanation of people going to church among ourselves. Admittedly, if rites are performed at critical times, as in sickness or at death, when the event which evokes them is one likely to occasion anxiety and distress, then these feelings will be present; but even here we have to be careful. The expression of emotion may be obligatory, an essential part of the rite itself, as in wailing and other signs of grief at death and funerals, whether the actors feel grief or not. In some societies professional mourners are employed. Then, again, if any emotional expression accompanies rites, it may well be that it is not the emotion which brings about the rites, but the rites which bring about the emotion. This is the old problem of whether we laugh because we are happy or are happy because we laugh. Surely we do not go to church because we are in a heightened emotional state, though our participation in the rites may bring about such a state.

Then, with regard to the alleged cathartic function of magic, what evidence is there that when a man performs agricultural, hunting, and fishing magic he feels frustrated, or that if he is in a state of tension the performance of the rites releases his distress? It seems to me that there is little or none. However he may be feeling, the magician has to perform the rites anyway, for they are a customary and obligatory part of the proceedings. It could with pertinence be said that primitive man performs his rites because he has faith in their efficacy, so that there is no great cause for frustration, since he knows that he has at hand the means of overcoming such difficulties as may present themselves. Rather than saying that magic releases tension, we might say that the possession of it prevents tension arising. Or, on the contrary, it could be said here again that, if there is any emotional state, it could well be, not the drive behind the rite, but the consequence of it, the gestures and spells producing the very psychological condition which is supposed to have led to the rite being performed. We have also to bear in mind that much magic and religion is vicarious, the magician or priest being a different person from the person on whose behalf the rite is performed, his client. So the person who is supposed to be in a state of tension is not the hired and disinterested person whose expletive gestures and words are supposed to release the tension. Therefore, if his gestures and spells suggest a heightened emotional state, it must either be simulated, or he must work himself into it during, and by, the rite. I might add that in Malinowski's case I think it is possible that much of his observation of rites was of those performed for his benefit, and in return for payment, quite outside their normal setting, in his tent; and if this is so, it could hardly be held that any display of emotion there may have been was caused by tension and frustration.

Furthermore, as Radin observed,[1] in an individual's experience the acquisition of rites and beliefs precedes the emotions which are said to accompany them later in adult life. He learns to participate in them before he experiences any emotion at all, so the emotional state, whatever it may be, and if there is one, can hardly be the genesis and explanation of them. A rite is part of the culture the individual is born into, and it imposes itself on him from the outside like the rest of his culture. It is a creation of society, not of individual reasoning or emotion, though it may satisfy both; and it is for this reason that Durkheim tells us that a psychological interpretation of a social fact is invariably a wrong interpretation.

For the same reason we must reject the wish-fulfilment theories. In comparing the neurotic with the magician they ignore the fact that the actions and formulas of the neurotic derive from individual subjective states, whereas those of the magician are traditional and socially imposed on him by his culture and society, part of the institutional framework in which he lives and to which he must conform; and, though in some instances and in some respects there may be certain outward resemblances, it cannot thereby be inferred that the psychological states are identical or that they stem from comparable conditions. In classing primitive peoples with children, neurotics, &c., the mistake is made of assuming that, because things may resemble each other in some particular feature, they are alike in other respects, the *pars pro toto* fallacy. All that it means is that, in the eyes of these writers,

---

[1] *Social Anthropology*, p. 247.

all these different sorts of people do not all the time think scientifically. And, we may ask, who ever met a savage who believed that by a thought of his he could change the world? He knows very well that he cannot. This is another variety of the 'if I were a horse' kind: if I were to behave in the way a savage magician does, I would be suffering from the maladies of my neurotic patients.

We are not, of course, to dismiss these interpretations out of hand. They were a not unhealthy reaction against a too intellectualist position. Desires and impulses, conscious and unconscious, motivate man, direct his interests, and impel him to action; and they certainly play their part in religion. That is not to be denied. What has to be determined is their nature and the part they do play. What I protest against is mere assertion, and what I challenge is an explanation of religion in terms of emotion or even, in the sway of it, of hallucination.

III

SOCIOLOGICAL THEORIES

THE emotionalist explanations of primitive religion which I have discussed have a strong pragmatist flavour. However foolish primitive beliefs and rites may appear to the rationalist mind, they help rude peoples to cope with their problems and misfortunes, and so they eradicate despair, which inhibits action, and make for confidence conducive to the individual's welfare, giving him a renewed sense of the value of life and of all the activities which promote it. Pragmatism was very influential at the time these explanations were being put forward, and Malinowski's theory of religion and magic might have come straight out of the pages of William James, as indeed it may have done: religion is valuable, even true in the pragmatist's sense of truth, if it serves the purpose of giving comfort and a feeling of security, confidence, relief, reassurance; if, that is, consequences useful to life flow from it. Among the writers about primitive thought so far mentioned, the pragmatist approach is perhaps most clearly enunciated by Carveth Read in a book earlier referred to. Why, he asks, is the human mind befogged with ideas of magic and religion? (He considered magic to be prior to religion, the origin of which is to be sought in dreams and belief in ghosts.) The answer is that, apart from the psychological relief they provide, in early stages of social evolution these superstitions were useful in giving support to leaders, and hence in sustaining order, government, and custom. Both are delusions, but natural selection favoured them. Totemic dances, we are told, 'give excellent physical training, promote the spirit of co-operation, are a sort of drill . . .'.[1] And much more on the same lines. We shall find that in general sociological theories of religion have the same flavour—religion is valuable in that it makes for social cohesion and continuity.

[1] Op. cit., p. 68.

This pragmatist way of regarding religion long antedates pragmatism as a formal philosophy. For example, Montesquieu, the father of social anthropology (though some might give the honour to Montaigne), tells us that though a religion may be false, it can have a most useful social function; and it will be found to conform to the type of government with which it is associated, a people's religion being in general suited to their way of life; which makes it difficult to transport a religion from one country to another. Thus function and veracity must not be confused. 'The most true and holy doctrines may be attended with the very worst consequences, when they are not connected with the principles of society; and, on the contrary, doctrines the most false may be attended with excellent consequences, when contrived so as to be connected with these principles.'[1] Even the ultra-rationalists of the Enlightenment, like Condorcet, conceded that religion, though false, had at one time a useful social function, and had therefore played an important role in the development of civilization.

Similar sociological insights are found in the earliest writings about human society. They are sometimes couched in what today would be called structural terms. Aristotle in the *Politics* says that 'all people say that the gods also had a king because they themselves had kings either formerly or now; for men create the gods after their own image, not only with regard to form; but also with regard to their manner of life'.[2] Hume says much the same; and we find this idea of a close connexion between political and religious development in several of our anthropological treatises. Herbert Spencer tells us that Zeus stands to the rest of the Celestials 'exactly in the same relation that an absolute monarch does to the aristocracy of which he is the head'.[3] Max Müller says that henotheism (a word, I believe, invented by him[4] to describe a religion in which each god, while he is being invoked, shares in all the attributes of a supreme being) arises in

---

[1] Montesquieu, *The Spirit of Laws*, 1750, ii. 161.
[2] i. 2. 7.   [3] Op. cit., i. 207.
[4] R. Pettazzoni, however, *Essays on the History of Religions*, 1954, p. 5, says that the word was first used by Schelling, the idea being later developed by Müller.

periods which precede the formation of nations out of independent tribes, it being a communal, as distinct from an imperial, form of religion. King also asserts that as political systems develop, their component parts are represented by tutelary gods; and when the parts become unified, when tribes aggregate into nations, the idea of a supreme being appears. He is the tutelary god of the dominant group in the amalgam. Finally comes monotheism, the supernal as a reflection of the universal, almighty, and eternal State. Robertson Smith explained the polytheism of classical antiquity in contrast to the monotheism of Asia by the fact that, in Greece and Rome, monarchy fell before the aristocracy, whereas in Asia it held its own: 'This diversity of political fortune is reflected in the diversity of religious development.'[1] Jevons follows the same line of reasoning. All this is a little naïve. Andrew Lang's writings and Wilhelm Schmidt's many volumes contain an abundance of evidence that peoples lacking political office, and therefore a political model for a supreme being, the hunters and collectors, are to a large extent monotheistic, at least in the sense of the word that there is only one god, though not in the sense that there is worship of one god and the denial of others (for there to be monotheism in the second sense—what has been called explicit monotheism—there has to be, or to have been, some form of polytheism).

Other examples of sociological analysis are to be found in the writings of Sir Henry Maine on comparative jurisprudence. He explains, for instance, the difference between Eastern and Western theology by the simple fact that in the West theology became combined with Roman jurisprudence, whereas no Greek-speaking society 'ever showed the smallest capacity for producing a philosophy of law'.[2] Theological speculation passed from a climate of Greek metaphysics to a climate of Roman law. But the most far-going and comprehensive sociological treatment of religion is Fustel de Coulanges's *The Ancient City*, and this French (Breton) historian is of particular interest to us because a pupil much

[1] W. Robertson Smith, *The Religion of the Semites*, 3rd edit. (1927), p. 73.
[2] H. S. Maine, *Ancient Law*, 1912 edit., p. 363.

influenced by him was Durkheim, whose theory of religion I am about to present. The theme of *The Ancient City* is that ancient classical society was centred in the family in a wide sense of that word—joint family or lineage—and that what held this group of agnates together as a corporation and gave it permanence was the ancestor cult, in which the head of the family acted as priest. In the light of this central idea, and only in the light of it, of the dead being deities of the family, all customs of the period can be understood: marriage regulations and ceremonies, monogamy, prohibition of divorce, interdiction of celibacy, the levirate, adoption, paternal authority, rules of descent, inheritance and succession, laws, property, the systems of nomenclature, the calendar, slavery and clientship, and many other customs. When city states developed, they were in the same structural pattern as had been shaped by religion in these earlier social conditions.

Another influence strongly marked in Durkheim's theory of religion, as also in the writings of F. B. Jevons, Salomon Reinach, and others, was that of the already-mentioned Robertson Smith, at one time Professor of Arabic at Cambridge. Taking some of his basic ideas from a fellow Scot, J. F. McLennan, he supposed that the Semitic societies of ancient Arabia were composed of matrilineal clans, each of which had a sacred relationship to a species of animal, their totem. The evidence for these suppositions is exiguous, but that is what Robertson Smith believed. Clansmen, according to him, were conceived to be of one blood, and their totems also; and of the same blood was the god of the clan, for he was thought of as the physical father of the founder of the clan. Sociologically speaking, the god was the clan itself, idealized and divinized. This projection had its material representation in the totemic creature; and the clan periodically expressed the unity of its members and of them with their god, and revitalized itself, by slaying the totemic creature and eating its raw flesh in a sacred feast, a communion 'in which the god and his worshippers unite by partaking together of the flesh and blood of a sacred victim'.[1] Now, since god, clansmen, and totem were all of one blood, the clansmen

[1] *The Religion of the Semites*, p. 227.

were partaking in a sacred communion not only with their god but also of their god, each member of the clan incorporating sacramentally a particle of the divine life into his own individual life. Later forms of Hebrew sacrifice developed out of this communion feast. The evidence for this theory, swallowed hook, line, and sinker by Jevons, is negligible; and it was, for a Presbyterian minister, getting rather near the bone, so either Robertson Smith himself, or whoever was responsible for the publication of the second and posthumous edition of *The Religion of the Semites* of 1894 (first edition: 1889), deleted certain passages which might be thought to discredit the New Testament.[1] All one can say of the theory as a whole, the argument of which is in the main both tortuous and tenuous, is that, whilst eating of the totem animal could have been the earliest form of sacrifice and the origin of religion, there is no evidence that it was. Moreover, in the vast literature on totemism throughout the world, there is only one instance, among the Australian aboriginals, of a people ceremonially eating their totems, and the significance of that instance, even if its veracity be accepted, is dubious and disputed. Apart from this, although Robertson Smith thought his theory to be generally true of primitive peoples, there are certainly many, including some of the most primitive, who lack bloody sacrifice altogether, and others among whom it is in no sense a communion. In this matter Robertson Smith misled both Durkheim and Freud.

It is also highly doubtful whether the idea of communion was at all present in the earliest form of Hebrew sacrifice known to us, and if it was, then there were also present, and perhaps more dominant, piacular and other ideas. Bluntly, all Robertson Smith really does is to guess about a period of Semitic history about which we know almost nothing. By doing so he may to some extent have made his theory safe from criticism, but to the same extent it thereby lacked cogency and conviction. Indeed, it was not historical at all, but an evolutionary theory, like all anthropological theories of the time, and this distinction must be clearly recognized. The evolutionary bias is conspicuous throughout, and is particularly

---

[1] J. G. Frazer, *The Gorgon's Head*, 1927, p. 289.

clear in his insistence on the materialistic crudity—what Preuss called *Urdummheit*—of primitive man's religion, thus placing the concrete, as opposed to the spiritual, at the beginning of development; and also laying undue stress on the social, as opposed to the personal, character of early religion; thereby revealing the basic assumption of all Victorian anthropologists, that the most primitive in thought and custom must be the antithesis of their own, their own in this case being a brand of individualistic spirituality.

To understand Robertson Smith's treatment of early Semitic religion and, by implication, of primitive religion in general, as well as, to a large extent, Durkheim's analysis, we have to note that he held that early religions lacked creeds and dogmas: 'they consisted entirely of institutions and practices.'[1] Rites, it is true, were connected with myths, but myths do not, for us, explain rites; rather the rites explain the myths. If this is so, then we must seek for an understanding of primitive religion in its ritual, and, since the basic rite in ancient religion is that of sacrifice, we must seek for it in the *sacrificium*; and further, since sacrifice is so general an institution, we must look for its origin in general causes.

Fundamentally, Fustel de Coulanges and Robertson Smith were putting forward what might be called a structural theory of the genesis of religion, that it arises out of the very nature of primitive society. This was also Durkheim's approach, and he proposed to show in addition the manner in which religion was generated. The position of Durkheim, perhaps the greatest figure in the history of modern sociology, can only be appraised if two points are kept in mind. The first is that for him religion is a social, that is an objective, fact. For theories which tried to explain it in terms of individual psychology he expressed contempt. How, he asked, if religion originated in a mere mistake, an illusion, a kind of hallucination, could it have been so universal and so enduring, and how could a vain fantasy have produced law, science, and morals? Animism is, in any case, in its developed and most typical forms, found not in primitive societies but in such relatively advanced societies as those of China, Egypt, and the classical

[1] *The Religion of the Semites*, p. 16.

Mediterranean. As for naturism (the nature-myth school), was religion to be explained any more satisfactorily as a disease of language, a muddle of metaphors, the action of language on thought, than as a false inference from dreams and trances? Apart from such an explanation being as trivial as the animistic one, it is a plain fact that primitive peoples show remarkably little interest in what we may regard as the most impressive phenomena of nature—sun, moon, sky, mountains, sea, and so forth—whose monotonous regularities they take very much for granted.[1] On the contrary, he claimed, in what he regarded as the most elementary religion of all, namely totemism, that what are divinized are for the most part not at all imposing, just humble little creatures like ducks, rabbits, frogs, and worms, whose intrinsic qualities could scarcely have been the origin of the religious sentiment they inspired.

It is true, of course, and Durkheim would certainly not have contested it, that religion is thought, felt, and willed by individuals—society has no mind to experience these functions—and as such it is a phenomenon of individual psychology, a subjective phenomenon, and can be studied accordingly. But it is none the less a social and objective phenomenon which is independent of individual minds, and it is as such that the sociologist studies it. What gives it objectivity are three characteristics. Firstly, it is transmitted from one generation to another, so if in one sense it is in the individual, in another it is outside him, in that it was there before he was born and will be there after he is dead. He acquires it as he acquires his language, by being born into a particular society. Secondly, it is, at any rate in a closed society, general. Everyone has the same sort of religious beliefs and practices, and their generality, or collectivity, gives them an objectivity which places them over and above the psychological experience of any individual, or indeed of all individuals. Thirdly, it is obligatory. Apart from positive and negative sanctions, the mere fact that religion is general means, again

[1] Hocart remarks, op. cit., *Man*, 1914, p. 99, that although in Fiji hurricanes are a yearly topic of conversation, he had never noticed 'the least suggestion of a native theory about them or the slightest tinge of religious awe'.

in a closed society, that it is obligatory, for even if there is no coercion, a man has no option but to accept what everybody gives assent to, because he has no choice, any more than of what language he speaks. Even were he to be a sceptic, he could express his doubts only in terms of the beliefs held by all around him. And had he been born into a different society, he would have had a different set of beliefs, just as he would have had a different language. It may here be noted that the interest shown by Durkheim and his colleagues in primitive societies may well have derived precisely from the fact that they are, or were, closed communities. Open societies, in which beliefs may not be transmitted and in which they are diversified, and therefore less obligatory, are less amenable to sociological interpretations on the lines pursued by them.

The second point which has to be borne in mind concerns the autonomy of religious phenomena. I will only mention it here since it emerges clearly from his treatment of religion, to which we are about to turn our attention. Durkheim was not nearly so deterministic and materialistic as some have made him out to be. Indeed, I should be inclined to regard him as a voluntarist and idealist. The functions of the mind could not exist without the processes of the organism, but that, he maintains, does not mean that psychological facts can be reduced to organic facts and be explained by them, but merely that they have an organic basis, just as organic processes have a chemical basis. At each level the phenomena have autonomy. Likewise, there could be no socio-cultural life without the psychical functions of individual minds, but social processes transcend these functions through which they, as it were, operate and, if not independent of mind, have an existence of their own outside individual minds. Language is a good example of what Durkheim was driving at. It is traditional, general, and obligatory; it has a history and structure and function of which those who speak it are quite unaware; and, though individuals may have contributed to it, it is certainly not the product of any individual's mind. It is a collective, autonomous, and objective phenomenon. In his analysis of religion Durkheim goes further. Religion is a social fact. It arises out of the nature of social life itself, being in the simpler societies bound up with other social facts, law, economics, art, &c., which later separate out from it and lead their own independent existences. Above all it is the way in which a society sees itself as more than a collection of individuals, and by which it maintains its solidarity and ensures its continuity. This does not mean, however, that it is merely an epiphenomenon of society, as the Marxists would have it. Once brought into existence by collective action, religion gains a degree of autonomy, and proliferates in all sorts of ways which cannot be explained by reference to the social structure which gave birth to it but only in terms of other religious and other social phenomena in a system all its own.

These two points having been made, we need delay no longer in presenting Durkheim's thesis. He started with four cardinal ideas taken from Robertson Smith, that primitive religion is a clan cult and that the cult is totemic (he thought that totemism and a clan segmentary system naturally imply each other), that the god of the clan is the clan itself divinized, and that totemism is the most elementary or primitive, and in that sense original, form of religion known to us. By that he meant that it is found in societies with the simplest material culture and social structure, and that it is possible to explain their religion without making use of any element borrowed from a previous religion. Durkheim thus agrees with those who see in totemism the origin of religion, or at least its earliest known form: McLennan, Robertson Smith, Wundt, Frazer in his earlier writings, Jevons, and Freud.

But what grounds are there for considering totemism to be a religious phenomenon at all? Frazer in his later writings put it in the category of magic. For Durkheim religion belongs to a broader class, the sacred; everything, real and ideal, belonging to one of two opposed classes, the profane and the sacred. The sacred is clearly identified by the fact that it is protected and isolated by interdictions, profane things being those to which these interdictions are applied. Taboo is here given much the same function as Marett gave it. Then, 'Religious beliefs are the representations which express the nature of sacred things', and rites are 'the rules of conduct which prescribe how a man should comport himself in the presence of sacred objects'.[1] These definitions cover both magic and religion in that they are both sacred on Durkheim's criterion, so he proposed a further criterion by which to distinguish between them. Religion is always a group, a collective, affair: there is no religion without a church. Magic has a clientele, not a church, the relationship between a magician and his client being comparable to that between a physician and his patient. So we arrive at a final definition of religion: 'A religion is a unified system of beliefs and practices relative to sacred things, that is to say, things set apart and forbidden—beliefs and practices which unite, into one single moral community called a church, all those who adhere to them.'[1] Durkheim's Hebraic background, it seems to me, comes out strongly, though not inappropriately, in this definition; but however that may be, on his criteria totemism can be regarded as a religion: it is hedged round by taboos, and it is a group manifestation.

What then is the object revered in this totemic religion? It is not simply a product of delirious imagination; it has an objective basis. It is a cult of something which really does exist, though not the thing the worshippers suppose. It is society itself, or some segment of it, which men worship in these ideal representations. And what, says Durkheim, is more natural, for a society has everything necessary to arouse the sensation of the divine in minds. It has absolute power over them, and it also gives them the feeling of perpetual dependence; and it is the object of venerable respect. Religion is thus a system of ideas by which individuals represent to themselves the society to which they belong and their relations with it.

Durkheim set out to prove his theory by taking the religion of some of the Australian aboriginals—using that of the North American Indians as a check—as a test case, holding that it was the simplest known form of religion. He defended this procedure by pleading with some justification that, in making a comparative study of social facts, they must be taken from

[1] E. Durkheim, *The Elementary Forms of the Religious Life*, English translation, n.d. [1915], p. 47.

societies of the same type, and that one well-controlled experiment is sufficient to establish a law, a piece of special pleading which seems to me to be little more than the ignoring of instances which contradict the so-called law. At the time the attention of anthropological writers was particularly engaged by recent discoveries made in Australia by the researches of Spencer and Gillen, Strehlow, and others. However, Durkheim's choice of that region for his experiment was unfortunate, for the literature on its aboriginals was, by modern standards, poor and confused, and it still is.

The Australian Blackfellows, as they used to be called, are (not many are left who live as they used to, but I retain the ethnographic present tense) hunters and collectors, wandering about in small hordes in their tribal territories seeking game, roots, fruits, grubs, and so forth. A tribe is composed of a number of such hordes. Besides being a member of a little horde and of the tribe in whose territory the horde lives, a person is a member of a clan, there being many such clans widely dispersed throughout the continent. As a member of his clan, he shares with its other members a relationship to a species of natural phenomena, mostly animals and plants. The species is sacred to the clan, and may not be eaten or harmed by its members. With each clan are classed other natural phenomena, so that the whole of nature belongs to one or other of the clans. The social structure thus provides the model for the classification of natural phenomena. Since the things so classed with the clans are associated with their totems, they also have a sacred character; and since the cults mutually imply each other, all are co-ordinated parts of a single religion, a tribal religion.

Durkheim acutely observed that the totemic creatures are not in any sense worshipped, as McLennan, Tylor, and Wundt seemed to think, nor, as I have earlier mentioned, had they been selected for their imposing appearance. Moreover, it is not the creatures themselves which are of first importance—they are sacred, it is true, but only secondarily so—but the designs of the creatures which are engraved on oblong pieces of wood or polished stone called *churinga*, sometimes pierced and used as bull roarers. Indeed, the totemic creatures had been selected, he would seem to suggest, because they were suitable models for pictorial representation. These designs are symbols in the first instance of an impersonal force distributed in images, animals, and men, but not to be confounded with any of them, for the sacred character of an object is not derived from its intrinsic properties; it is added to them, superimposed on them. Totemism is a kind of impersonal god immanent in the world and diffused in an innumerable multitude of things, corresponding to *mana* and similar ideas among primitive peoples: the *wakan* and *orenda* of the North American Indians, for example. However, the Australians conceive of it, not in an abstract form, but in the form of an animal or plant, the totem, which is 'the material form under which the imagination represents this immaterial substance'.[1] Since this essence, or vital principle, is found in both men and their totems, and is for both their most essential characteristic, we can understand what a Blackfellow means when he says that the men of the Crow phratry, for example, are crows.

The designs symbolize in the second instance the clans themselves. The totem is at once both the symbol of the god, or vital principle, and of the society, because god and society are the same thing. 'The god of the clan, the totemic principle, can therefore be nothing else than the clan itself, personified and represented to the imagination under the visible form of the animal or vegetable which serves as totem.'[2] In the totemic symbols clansmen express their moral identity and their feelings of dependence on each other and on the group as a whole. People can only communicate by signs, and to communicate this feeling of solidarity a symbol, a flag, is required, and it is provided for these natives by their totems, each clan expressing both its unity and its exclusiveness in its totemic emblem. Concrete symbols are necessary because 'the clan is too complex a reality to be represented clearly in all its complex unity by such rudimentary intelligences'.[3] Unsophisticated minds cannot think of themselves as a social group except through material symbols. The totemic principle is thus nothing else than the clan thought of under

---

[1] Op. cit., p. 189.   [2] Ibid., p. 206.   [3] Ibid., p. 220.

the material form of the totemic emblem. By the manner in which it acts upon its members, the clan awakens within them the idea of external forces which dominate and exalt them, and these external forces are represented by external things, the totemic forms. The sacred is no more, and it is also no less, than society itself, represented in symbols to its members.

Durkheim recognized that the Australian aboriginals had religious conceptions other than what is labelled totemism, but he held that they were equally explicable in terms of his theory. The idea of the soul is nothing more than the totemic principle, *mana*, incarnate in each individual, society individualized. It is his society in each member of it, its culture and social order, that which makes a man a person, a social being instead of a mere animal. It is the social personality as distinct from the individual organism. Man is a rational and moral animal, but the rational and moral part of him is what society has superimposed on the organic part. As Miss Harrison, paraphrasing Durkheim, put it, 'His body obeys natural law and his spirit is bound by the social imperative'.[1] Therefore the soul is not the product of pure illusion, as Tylor and others would have it. We *are* made up of two distinct parts, which are opposed to one another as the sacred to the profane. Society does not just move us from without and for the moment. 'It establishes itself within us in a durable manner. . . . So we are really made up of two beings facing in different and almost contrary directions, one of whom exercises a real pre-eminence over the other. Such is the profound meaning of the antithesis which all men have more or less clearly conceived between the body and the soul, the material and spiritual beings who coexist within us . . . our nature is double; there really is a particle of divinity in us because there is within us a particle of these great ideas which are the soul of the group.'[2] There is nothing derogatory for religion or for man in this interpretation. On the contrary, 'The only way

[1] J. E. Harrison, *Themis. A Study of the Social Origins of Greek Religion*, 1912, p. 487. The book was published in the same year as Durkheim's *Les Formes élémentaires de la vie religieuse*. Miss Harrison had been influenced by his earlier 'De la définition des phénomènes religieux,' *L'Année sociologique*, ii (1899).

[2] Durkheim, *The Elementary Forms of the Religious Life*, pp. 262–4.

we have of freeing ourselves from physical forces is to oppose them with collective forces'.[1] Man then, as Engels put it, ascends from the kingdom of necessity to the kingdom of freedom.

As for the Australian spiritual beings, a notion Durkheim, like Tylor, thought to be derived from that of the soul, they seem, he believed, to have been totems at one time. However that may be, they now correspond to tribal groups. In each territory many clans are represented, each with its distinctive totemic emblems and cults, but all alike belong also to the tribe and have the same religion, and this tribal religion is idealized in the gods. The great god is simply the synthesis of all the totems, just as the tribes are syntheses of all the clans represented in them; and it is inter-tribal also in character, mirroring social relations between tribe and tribe, especially the assistance of members of other tribes at tribal ceremonies of initiation and sub-incision. So while souls and spirits do not exist in reality, they correspond to reality and in that sense they are real, for the social life they symbolize is real enough.

So far nothing has been said about the ritual side of Australian totemism; and here we come to the central and most obscure part of Durkheim's thesis, and also the most unconvincing part of it. Periodically members of the same clan, presumably for the most part members of the same tribe, meet together to perform ceremonies to increase the species to which they have a sacred relationship. Since they may not eat their own totemic creatures, the rites are intended to benefit members of other clans who may eat them, all the clans thus making their contribution to the common food-supply. So the aboriginals state the purpose of the rites, but manifest purpose and latent function are not the same; and Durkheim has a sociological interpretation of their performances which does not at all accord with their own idea of what they are doing, if indeed that is the purpose of the ceremonies for them, which does not seem to be certain. That the ceremonies, called *intichiuma*, are not really concerned with increasing the species, that this is a rationalization, is shown, says

[1] Ibid., p. 272.

Durkheim, by the fact that they are performed even when a totem, the *wollunqua*, is a non-existent snake which is thought to be unique and also not to reproduce itself, and by the further fact that precisely the same ceremony which is said to increase the species can be held at initiation and on other occasions. Such rites serve only to awaken certain ideas and sentiments, to attach the present to the past and the individual to the group. Their stated purpose is wholly accessory and contingent, as is further shown in that sometimes even the beliefs which attribute a physical efficaciousness to the rites are lacking, without causing any alterations in their essentials.

Rationalist theorists of religion have generally treated conceptions and beliefs as the essentials of religion, and regarded the rites as only an external translation of these. But, as we have already heard from others, it is action which dominates the religious life. Durkheim writes:

We have seen that if collective life awakens religious thought on reaching a certain degree of intensity, it is because it brings about a state of effervescence which changes the conditions of psychic activity. Vital energies are over-excited, passions more active, sensations stronger; there are even some which are produced only at this moment. A man does not recognize himself; he feels himself transformed and consequently he transforms the environment which surrounds him. In order to account for the very particular impressions which he receives, he attributes to the things with which he is in most direct contact properties which they have not, exceptional powers and virtues which the objects of every-day experience do not possess. In a word, above the real world where his profane life passes he has placed another which, in one sense, does not exist except in thought, but to which he attributes a higher sort of dignity than to the first. Thus, from a double point of view it is an ideal world.[1]

For a society to become conscious of itself and to maintain its sentiments at the necessary degree of intensity, it must periodically assemble and concentrate itself. This concentration brings about an exaltation of the mental life, which takes the form of a group of ideal conceptions.

So it is not the stated purpose of the rites which tells us their function. Their real significance is, firstly, that they draw

[1] Durkheim, *The Elementary Forms of the Religious Life*, p. 422.

clansmen together, and secondly, that the collective enactment of the rites on these occasions of concentration renews
in them a feeling of solidarity. The rites generate an effervescence, in which all sense of individuality is lost and people
feel themselves as a collectivity in and through their sacred
things. But when the clansmen separate, the sense of solidarity
slowly runs down, and has to be recharged from time to time
by another assembly and repetition of the ceremonies, in
which the group once again reaffirms itself. Even if men
believe that the rites act on things, it is in fact alone the mind
which is acted on. It will be noted that Durkheim is not saying here, like the emotionalist writers, that the rites are performed to release some heightened emotional state. It is the
rites which produce such a state. They may therefore, in this
respect, be compared to the piacular rites, such as those of
mourning, in which people make expiation to affirm their
faith and to fulfil a duty to society, and not because of some
emotional condition, which may be totally lacking.

Such was Durkheim's theory. For Freud God is the
father, for Durkheim God is society. Now, if his theory holds
for the Australian aboriginals, it holds good for religion in
general, for, he says, totemic religion contains all the elements
of other religions, even those the most advanced. Durkheim
was candid enough to admit this, that what is sauce for the
goose is sauce for the gander. If the idea of sacredness, of
the soul and of God, can be explained sociologically for the
Australians, then in principle the same explanation is valid
for all peoples among whom the same ideas are found with
the same essential characteristics. Durkheim was most anxious
not to be accused of a mere restatement of historical materialism. In showing that religion is something essentially social
he does not mean that collective consciousness is a mere epiphenomenon of its morphological basis, just as individual
consciousness is not merely an efflorescence of the nervous
system. Religious ideas are produced by a synthesis of individual minds in collective action, but once produced
they have a life of their own: the sentiments, ideas, and
images 'once born, obey laws all their own'.[1] None the less, if

[1] Ibid., p. 424.

Durkheim's theory of religion is true, obviously no one is going to accept religious beliefs any more; and yet, on his own showing, they are generated by the action of social life itself, and are necessary for its persistence. This put him on the horns of a dilemma, and all he could say to get off them was that, while religion in the spiritual sense is doomed, a secular assembly may produce ideas and sentiments which will have the same function; and in support of this opinion, he cites the French revolution with its cult of Fatherland, Liberty, Equality and Fraternity, and Reason. Did it not in its first years make these ideas into sacred things, into gods, and the society it had brought into being a god? He hoped and expected, like Saint-Simon and Comte, that as spiritual religion declined, a secularistic religion of a humanist kind would take its place.

Durkheim's thesis is more than just neat; it is brilliant and imaginative, almost poetical; and he had an insight into a psychological fundamental of religion: the elimination of the self, the denial of individuality, its having no meaning, or even existence, save as part of something greater, and other, than the self. But I am afraid that we must once more say that it is also a just-so story. Totemism could have arisen through gregariousness, but there is no evidence that it did; and other forms of religion could have developed, as it is implicit in Durkheim's theory that they did, from totemism, or what he calls the totemic principle, but again there is no evidence that they did. It can be allowed that religious conceptions must bear some relation to the social order, and be in some degree in accord with economic, political, moral, and other social facts, and even that they are a product of social life, in the sense that there could be no religion without society, any more than there could be thought or culture of any kind; but Durkheim is asserting much more than that. He is claiming that spirit, soul, and other religious ideas and images are projections of society, or of its segments, and originate in conditions bringing about a state of effervescence.

My comments must be few and brief. While various logical and philosophical objections could be raised, I would rather base the case for the prosecution on ethnographical evidence. Does this support the rigid dichotomy he makes between the sacred and the profane? I doubt it. Surely what he calls 'sacred' and 'profane' are on the same level of experience, and, far from being cut off from one another, they are so closely intermingled as to be inseparable. They cannot, therefore, either for the individual or for social activities, be put in closed departments which negate each other, one of which is left on entering the other. For instance, when some misfortune such as sickness is believed to be due to some fault, the physical symptoms, the moral state of the sufferer, and the spiritual intervention form a unitary objective experience, and can scarcely be separated in the mind. My test of this sort of formulation is a simple one: whether it can be broken down into problems which permit testing by observation in field research, or can at least aid in a classification of observed facts. I have never found that the dichotomy of sacred and profane was of much use for either purpose.

It may be suggested here also that Durkheim's definitions did not allow for situational flexibility, that what is 'sacred' may be so only in certain contexts and on certain occasions, and not in other situations and on other occasions. This point has been mentioned earlier. I give here a single example. The Zande cult of ancestors is centred round shrines erected in the middle of their courtyards, and offerings are placed in these shrines on ceremonial, and sometimes other, occasions; but when not in ritual use, so to speak, Azande use them as convenient props to rest their spears against, or pay no attention to them whatsoever. Also, the demarcation of the 'sacred' by interdictions may be true of a great many peoples, but it cannot be universally valid, as Durkheim supposed, if I am right in believing that the participants in the elaborate sacrificial rites of the Nilotic peoples, or some of them, are not subjected to any interdictions.

With regard to the Australian evidence cited: one of the weaknesses of Durkheim's position is the plain fact that among the Australian aboriginals it is the horde, and then the tribe, which are the corporate groups, and not the widely dispersed clans; so if the function of religion is to maintain the solidarity of the groups which most require a sense of unity, then it should be the hordes and tribes, and not the clans, that should perform the rites generating effervescence.[1] Durkheim saw this point, and tried to elude it by the answer, which seems to me to be inadequate, that it is precisely because the clans lack cohesion, having neither chiefs nor a common territory, that periodic concentrations are necessary. What is the point of maintaining through ceremonies the solidarity of social groupings which are not corporate and which do not have any joint action outside the ceremonies?

Durkheim chose to argue his thesis on the evidence of totemism, and almost entirely on that of Australian totemism. Now, Australian totemism is a very untypical and highly specialized type of totemism, and conclusions drawn from it, even if accurate, cannot be taken as valid for totemism in general. Furthermore, totemic phenomena are by no means the same throughout Australia. Durkheim was highly selective in his choice of material, restricting himself in the main to that of Central Australia and mostly to that of the Arunta. His theory does not take into consideration that, in other parts of the continent, the *intichiuma* ceremonies appear to have a very different significance and not the same importance, or are even lacking altogether. Then, totemism among other peoples lacks the features Durkheim most stresses, such as concentrations, ceremonies, sacred objects, designs, &c. The defence that totemism elsewhere is a more developed institution or the institution in decay is a plea we cannot allow, for there is no means of knowing anything about the history of totemism in Australia or elsewhere. The assertion that Australian totemism is the original form of totemism is quite arbitrary, and rests on the assumption that the simplest form of religion is necessarily held by people with the simplest culture and social organization. But even if we accept this criterion, we would then have to account for the fact that some hunting and collecting peoples, as technologically undeveloped as the Australians and with a much simpler

[1] It must be remarked that the terminology for the Australian aboriginal political groups is not just ambiguous, it is chaotic. It is difficult to know precisely what is meant by 'tribe', 'clan', 'nation', 'horde', 'family', &c. See G. C. W. Wheeler, *The Tribe and Intertribal Relations in Australia*, 1910, *passim.*

social organization, have no totems (or clans), or their totems are of no great importance for them, and yet they have religious beliefs and rites. It might be pointed out also that for Durkheim totemism was essentially a clan religion, a product of this kind of social segmentation, and that therefore where there are clans, they are totemic, and where there is totemism, the society has a clan organization, an assumption in which he was mistaken, for there are peoples with clans and no totems, and peoples with totems and no clans.[1] As a matter of fact, as Goldenweiser has pointed out, Durkheim's assertion that the social organization of the Australians is on a basis of clans is quite contrary to the ethnographical evidence, and this by itself makes his whole theory questionable.[2] Then, by placing the emphasis on figured representations of the totemic creatures, Durkheim also laid himself open to the damaging observations that most of the totems are not, in fact, figured representationally. One must say also that there appears to be precious little evidence that the gods of Australia are syntheses of totems; though this is a clever attempt to get rid of their awkward presence. One sometimes sighs—if only Tylor, Marett, Durkheim, and all the rest of them could have spent a few weeks among the peoples about whom they so freely wrote!

I have mentioned a few points which seem to me to be sufficient to raise doubts about Durkheim's theory, if not to invalidate it altogether. More could be cited, and they are to be found in Van Gennep's devastating criticisms, all the more vigorous and caustic in that Durkheim and his colleagues excluded and ignored him.[3] I must, however, before passing rapidly in review some constructions closely related to the one we have been discussing, make a final comment on his theory of the genesis of totemism and therefore of religion in general. It contravenes his own rules of sociological method, for fundamentally it offers a psychological explanation of

---

[1] Lowie, *Primitive Society*, 1921, p. 137.

[2] Goldenweiser, 'Religion and Society: A Critique of Émile Durkheim's Theory of the Origin and Nature of Religion', *Journal of Philosophy, Psychology and Scientific Methods*, xii (1917).

[3] A. Van Gennep, *L'État actuel du problème totémique*, 1920, pp. 40 ff.

social facts, and he himself has laid it down that such explana-tions are invariably wrong. It was all very well for him to pour contempt on others for deriving religion from motor hallucination, but I contend that this is precisely what he does himself. No amount of juggling with words like 'inten-sity' and 'effervescence' can hide the fact that he derives the totemic religion of the Blackfellows from the emotional excitement of individuals brought together in a small crowd, from what is a sort of crowd hysteria. Some of our earlier objections, and for the matter of that Durkheim's too, must therefore stand here also. What is the evidence that the Blackfellows are in any particular emotional state during the performance of their ceremonies? And if they are, then it is evident that the emotion is produced, as Durkheim himself claimed, by the rites and the beliefs which occasion them, so the rites and beliefs which occasion them cannot convin-cingly be adduced as a product of the emotions. Therefore heightened emotion, whatever it may be, and if there is any particular emotional state associated with the ritual, could indeed be an important element in the rites, giving them a deeper significance for the individual, but it can hardly be an adequate causal explanation of them as a social phenomenon. The argument, like so many sociological argu-ments, is a circular one—the chicken and the egg. The rites create the effervescence, which creates the beliefs, which cause the rites to be performed; or does the mere coming together generate them? Fundamentally Durkheim elicits a social fact from crowd psychology.

Indeed, it is not a long jump from Durkheim's theory—though he would have been shocked had he heard it said —to a biological explanation of religion, such as Trotter appears to offer: it is a by-product of the herd instinct, the instinct of gregariousness, one of the four instincts which bulk largely in man's life, the other three being those of self-preservation, nutrition, and sex. I say that this is the thesis Trotter appears to offer, because on this topic he is not very precise: the intimate dependence on the herd 'compels the individual to reach out towards some larger existence than his own, some encompassing being in whom his complexities may find a solution and his longings peace'.[1] Trotter's book is, however, more a moral polemic than a scientific study. Nevertheless, one may note in it the same idealistic (socialistic) fervour which informs Durkheim's book.

Some of the ideas found in Durkheim's volume were developed by his colleagues, students, and others influenced by him. If I review only some of them, and those cursorily, it is because these lectures are intended to illustrate different ways of looking at a subject or a problem, and not to be a complete history of ideas, or a comprehensive catalogue of writers about them. One of the best-known essays in the journal which Durkheim founded and edited, *L'Année sociologique*, was a study of the literature on the Eskimoes by his nephew Marcel Mauss (in collaboration with M. H. Beuchat).[2] The general theme of this essay was a demonstration of Durkheim's thesis that religion is a product of social concentration and is kept alive by periodic gregariousness, so that time, like things, has sacred and secular dimensions. We need not enter into details: suffice it that he showed how the Eskimoes, during that part of the year (the summer) when the seas are free from ice, are dispersed in small family groups living in tents. When the ice forms they are no longer able to pursue game, so they spend this part of the year (the winter) in larger and more concentrated groups living in long houses, a number of different families sharing a common room, so that then people are involved in a wider set of social relations, the social order thus being not only of a different proportion, but also of a different arrangement or order or structure, for the community is then not just a number of families living together for convenience, but a new form of social grouping in which individuals are related on a different pattern. With this changed pattern we find a different set of laws, morals, and, in general, customs, suited to it, which do not operate during the period of dispersal. It is when these larger groups form that the annual religious ceremonies are performed; so it

---

[1] W. Trotter, *Instincts of the Herd in Peace and War*, 5th impression (1920), p. 113.

[2] M. Mauss, 'Essai sur les variations saisonnières des sociétés eskimos: Étude de morphologie sociale', *L'Année sociologique*, ix (1906).

could be held that the Eskimoes are a confirmatory illustration of Durkheim's theory.[1]

However ingenious this exposition may be, it demonstrates little more than that, for the performance of religious ceremonies, leisure and a sufficient number of people to take part in them are required. Also, the case is very different from that of the Australian aboriginals, where clansmen come together periodically to perform their totemic ceremonies. The Eskimoes come together for different reasons, and they only disperse from necessity. Mauss, like Durkheim, held that a law can be formulated on one well-controlled experiment, but such a formulation is not a law but an hypothesis; and it happens that I have myself studied a people, the Nuer, among whom the period of greater concentration is not that in which ceremonies are held, for reasons which are chiefly a matter of convenience.

In another essay in the *Année* Mauss, together with that fine historian Henri Hubert, had earlier distinguished magic from religion as Durkheim did, and had made an exhaustive study of that part of the sacred, the magical,[2] which Durkheim did not treat in his *The Elementary Forms of the Religious Life*; and the same pair of scholars had yet earlier published, in the same journal, a masterly analysis of Vedic and Hebrew sacrifice.[3] But, masterly though it was, its conclusions are an unconvincing piece of sociologistic metaphysics. Gods are representations of communities, they are societies thought of ideally and imaginatively. So the renunciations in sacrifice nourish social forces—mental and moral energies. Sacrifice is an act of abnegation by which the individual recognizes society; it recalls to particular consciences the presence of collective forces, represented by their gods. But though the act of abnegation implicit in any sacrifice

---

[1] Mauss's essay was published before Durkheim's *Les Formes élémentaires de la vie religieuse*, but Durkheim had set forth his views earlier than in that book; and the two men's researches and writings were so intertwined that it is impossible to disentangle them.

[2] H. Hubert and M. Mauss, 'Esquisse d'une théorie générale de la magie', *L'Année sociologique*, vii (1904).

[3] H. Hubert and M. Mauss, 'Essai sur la nature et la fonction du sacrifice', *L'Année sociologique*, ii (1899).

serves to sustain collective forces, the individual finds advantage in the same act, because in it the whole strength of society is conferred on him, and it also provides the means of redressing equilibria that have been upset; a man redeems himself by expiation from social obloquy, a consequence of error, and re-enters the community. Thus the social function of sacrifice is fulfilled, both for the individual and for the collectivity. All this seems to me to be a mixture of mere assertion, conjecture, and reification, for which no satisfactory evidence is adduced. They are conclusions not deriving from, but posited on, a brilliant analysis of the mechanism of sacrifice, or perhaps one should say of its logical structure, or even of its grammar.

I mention also, as examples of sociological method, two remarkable essays by a younger member of the *Année* group, Robert Hertz.[1] In one of these he relates Durkheim's dichotomy of sacred and profane to the ideas of right and left, represented by the two hands, which all over the world stand for opposites, the right for goodness, virtue, strength, masculinity, the east, life, &c., and the left for the contraries. The other essay is an attempt to explain why so many peoples have not only disposal of the dead, which is easily intelligible, but also further mortuary ceremonies, and in particular the custom, prevalent in Indonesia, of double disposal of the dead. The body is first placed in a temporary abode by itself, where it rests till the body has decomposed, when the bones are collected and placed in the 'family' ossuary. This procedure represents, in the material symbol of the decomposing body, the lengthy passage of the soul of the dead from the world of the living to the world of the ghosts, a transition from one status to another, and the two movements correspond to a third one, the release of the survivors from their attachment to the dead. At the second obsequies all three articulated movements reach a concerted climax and termination. They are really different facets of a single process, the adjustment of society to the loss of one of its members, a slow process, because people do not readily reconcile themselves to death as either a physical or moral fact.

[1] R. Hertz, *Death and the Right Hand*, 1960.

In England sociological theories of religion, and especially the Durkheimian one, greatly influenced a generation of classical scholars—Gilbert Murray, A. B. Cook, Francis Cornford, and others—as is clearly acknowledged by Jane Harrison, who accounts for Greek religion, and by implication all religion, in terms of collective feeling and thinking. It is the product of effervescence induced by ceremonial activity, the projection of group emotion, the ecstasy of a group (*thiasos*). Although she confesses that savages 'weary and disgust me, though perforce I spend long hours in reading of their tedious doings', she transplants on Greek soil the supposed mentality of the Australian aboriginals; and there in Greek form we find all the old plums. Sacraments 'can only be understood in the light of totemistic thinking . . .'.[1] Greek religious phenomena 'depend on, or rather express and represent, the social structure of the worshippers'.[2] 'Social structure and the collective conscience which utters itself in social structure, underlie all religion.'[3] 'Bacchic religion is based on the collective emotion of the *thiasos*. Its god is a projection of group-unity. Dr. Verrall in his essay on the *Bacchants of Euripides* hits the mark in one trenchant, illuminating bit of translation, "The rapture of the initiated", he says, lies essentially in this: "*his soul is congregationalized*".'[4] Man also reacts collectively to the universe: 'We have seen his emotion extend itself, project itself into natural phenomena, and noted how this projection begets in him such conceptions as *mana, orenda* . . .'[5] (with which are equated the Greek conceptions of power (*kratos*) and force (*bia*)). Totemism is 'a phase or stage of collective thinking through which the human mind is bound to pass'.[6] Both sacrament and sacrifice are 'only special forms of that manipulation of *mana* which we have agreed to call magic'.[7] 'Religion has in it then two elements, social custom, the collective conscience, and the emphasis and representation of that collective conscience. It has in a word within it two factors indissolubly linked: ritual, this is custom, collective action, and myth or theology,

---

[1] Harrison, op. cit., p. xii.　　　　　　　　[2] Ibid., p. xvii.
[3] Ibid., p. xviii.　　　　[4] Ibid., p. 48.　　[5] Ibid., pp. 73–74.
[6] Ibid., p. 122.　　　　　　　　　　　　　　[7] Ibid., p. 134.

the representation of the collective emotion, the collective conscience. And—a point of supreme importance—both are incumbent, binding, and interdependent.'[1]

The flaws in Durkheim's theory, due mainly to his pursuit of the genesis, the origin, and the cause of religion, are accentuated if anything even more in the writings of another well-known classical scholar, Francis Cornford, who also acknowledges his debt to Durkheim. For him, too, the individual does not count, save as an organism, in the most primitive communities. In other respects only the group counts; and the world of nature is categorized on the pattern of the structure of the social group. As for religion, souls and gods of one sort or another are merely representations of the same structure. In both cases, the way nature is conceived of and religious beliefs, the categories of thought are projections of the collective mind. The soul is the collective soul of the group; it is society itself, which is both in and outside any individual member of it; and hence it is immortal because, although its individual members die, the society itself is immortal. From the notion of soul the representation of a god develops when a certain degree of political complexity, individualization, and sophistication has been attained. Ultimately, however, all religious representations are an illusion by what Cornford calls herd-suggestion. So he concludes that 'the first religious representation is a representation of the collective consciousness itself—the only moral power which can come to be felt as imposed from without, and therefore need to be represented'.[2]

Valuable though the influence of the sociological, and especially Durkheim's, approach to religion may have been in suggesting new ways of looking at the facts of classical antiquity, it must be admitted that such statements as those I have cited are little more than conjecture, indeed that they go far beyond the bounds of legitimate speculation. The evidence in support of them is by any critical standard both meagre and doubtful.

The main exponent in more recent times of a sociological interpretation of primitive religion on this side of the Channel

[1] Ibid., p. 486. [2] F. M. Cornford, *From Religion to Philosophy*, 1912, p. 82.

was the English Durkheimian (though I believe he owed as much, or more, to Herbert Spencer) A. R. Radcliffe-Brown.[1] He tried to restate Durkheim's theory of totemism to make it more comprehensive,[2] though in doing so, in my opinion, he made nonsense of it. He wished to show that totemism was only a special form of a phenomenon universal in human society, it being a general law that any object or event which has important effects on the material or spiritual well-being of a society tends to become an object of the ritual attitude (a very dubious generalization). So people who depend on hunting and collecting for their survival have a ritual attitude to the animals and plants most useful to them. Totemism arises from this general attitude when social segmentation takes place. In his discussion of totemism, Radcliffe-Brown steered clear of Durkheim's explanation of its genesis in crowd psychology; but elsewhere, for example in his account of dancing among the Andaman Islanders, he takes up much the same position.[3] In the dance, he tells us, the personality of the individual submits to the action upon him by the community, and the harmonious concert of individual feelings and actions produces a maximum unity and concord of the community which is intensely felt by every individual member of it. That may, or may not, be the case among the Andamanese, but in one of my earliest papers I felt bound to protest against its acceptance as a generalization, for the dances I had observed in Central Africa were one of the most frequent occasions of disharmony, and my subsequent experience has confirmed my youthful scepticism.

A chain is tested by its weakest link. We see in Radcliffe-Brown's writings how unsatisfactory this sort of sociological explanation of religious phenomena can be. In one of his last public lectures, the Henry Myres Lecture,[4] he says that

[1] It is important in assessing Radcliffe-Brown's position to know that he finished his research among the Andaman Islanders before he had become acquainted with Durkheim's writings, under the influence of which he published the results of the research.

[2] A. R. Radcliffe-Brown, 'The Sociological Theory of Totemism', *Fourth Pacific Science Congress*, Java, 1929, iii, Biological Papers, pp. 295–309.

[3] Idem, *The Andaman Islanders*, 1922, pp. 246 ff.

[4] Idem, 'Religion and Society', *Journal of the Royal Anthropological Institute*, lxxv (1945).

religion is everywhere an expression of a sense of dependence on a spiritual or moral power outside ourselves: surely, Schleiermacher and other philosophers apart, a commonplace from any pulpit. But Radcliffe-Brown was attempting to formulate a sociological proposition that goes far beyond this rather vague general statement. If Durkheim's thesis were to be proved, it would have to be shown that the conception of the divine varies according to the different forms of societies, a task Durkheim did not undertake. So, says Radcliffe-Brown, since religion has the function of maintaining the solidarity of society, it must vary in form with types of social structure. In societies with a lineage system we may expect to find ancestor cult. The Hebrews and the city states of Greece and Rome had national religions in conformity with their types of political structure. This is really saying, as Durkheim said, that the entities postulated by religion are no more than society itself, and the reasoning is at best no more than plausible. Where it ceases to be a statement of the obvious it is only too often contradicted by the facts: for example, ancestor cult is often the religion of peoples lacking lineages, as among many African peoples; and perhaps the most perfect example of a lineage system is that of the Bedouin Arabs, who are Muslims. And have not both Christianity and Islam been adopted by peoples with quite different types of social structure?

There are grave objections to all the sort of sociological (or should we say sociologistic?) explanations we have been considering, not the least being the inadequacy of the data, which, as I have earlier said, are often confused and confusing. Then, we have here to urge again, negative instances cannot just be ignored. They must be accounted for in terms of the theory put forward, or the theory must be abandoned. What about primitive peoples who have clans and no totems; who have belief in the survival of the soul but no second obsequies or mortuary rites; who do not associate the right orientation with superior moral qualities; who have lineages but no ancestor cult; &c.? By the time all the exceptions have been registered and somehow accounted for, the remains of the theories are little more than plausible guesses of so general and vague a character that they are of little scientific value, all the more so in that nobody knows what to do with them, since they can neither be proved nor disproved in final analysis. If one were to test the theory of Durkheim and of Mauss about the origin and meaning of religion, how could it be either substantiated or shown to be wrong? If one were to challenge Hertz's explanation of double obsequies, how could it be upheld, or for the matter of that shown to be untrue? How does one know whether religion maintains or does not maintain the solidarity of a society? All these theories may be true, but equally they may be false. Neat and consistent they may appear to be, but they tend to stultify further inquiry, because in so far as they go beyond description of the facts and offer explanations of them, they do not easily permit experimental verification. The supposition that a certain kind of religion goes with, or is the product of, a certain type of social structure would only have a high degree of probability if it could be shown historically not only that changes in social structure have caused corresponding changes in religious thought, but also that it is a regular correspondence; or if it could be shown that all societies of a certain type have similar religious systems, which was an axiom for Lévy-Bruhl, whose contribution to the discussion will be the subject of the next lecture.

In concluding this one, passing attention might be called to the similarity some of the theories we have touched on bear to those of Marxist writers, or some of them, who in many ways present the most straightforward and lucid exposition of a sociological point of view. Religion is a form of social 'superstructure', it is a 'mirror' or a 'reflection' of social relations, which themselves rest upon the basic economic structure of society. The notions of 'spirit', 'soul', &c., derive from a time when there were clan leaders, patriarchs, 'in other words, when the division of labor led to the segregation of administrative work'.[1] Hence, religion begins with worship of ancestors, of the elders of the clan: in origin it is 'a reflection of production relations (particularly those of master and servant) and the *political order of society* conditioned

[1] N. Bukharin, *Historical Materialism. A System of Sociology*, 1925, p. 170.

by them'.[1] So, religion tends always to take the form of the economico-political structure of society, though there may be a time-lag in the adjustment of the one to the other. In a society consisting of loosely connected clans religion assumes the form of polytheism; where there is a centralized monarchy, there is a single god; where there is a slave-holding commercial republic (as at Athens in the sixth century B.C.), the gods are organized as a republic. And so forth. It is, of course, true that religious conceptions can only be derived from experience, and the experience of social relations must furnish a model for such conceptions. Such a theory may, at least sometimes, account for the conceptual forms taken by religion, but not for its origin, its function, or its meaning. In any case, neither ethnography nor history (e.g. it is quite untrue that, as Bukharin asserts, in the Reformation the ruling princes all sided with the Pope)[2] sustains the thesis.

Though I cannot discuss the matter further here, I would suggest that in their general approach to the study of social phenomena there is much in common, though they are dressed differently, between the French sociological school and the Marxist theorists. Though the latter regarded Durkheim as a bourgeois idealist, he might well have written Marx's famous aphorism, that it is not the consciousness of men that determines their being but their social being which determines their consciousness. Bukharin quotes Lévy-Bruhl, to whom we next turn, with apparent approval.

[1] Ibid., pp. 170–1.
[2] Ibid., p. 178.

IV

LÉVY-BRUHL

No account of theories of primitive religion would be adequate which did not devote special and separate attention to Lévy-Bruhl's voluminous writings on primitive mentality, an expression which derives from the title of one of his books, *La Mentalité primitive*. His conclusions about the nature of primitive thought were for many years a matter of lively controversy, and most anthropologists of the day felt constrained to take a swipe at him. After setting forth and criticizing his opinions, I shall make a brief review of what Pareto has to offer to our deliberations, partly because he is a useful foil to Lévy-Bruhl, and partly because what he has to say serves as a convenient bridge into the general discussion and summary which follow.

Lévy-Bruhl was a philosopher who had already made a big reputation by outstanding books on Jacobi and Comte before he turned his attention, as had his contemporary Durkheim, also a philosopher, to the study of primitive man. The publication of his *La Morale et la science des moeurs* in 1903 marks the change in his interests towards the study of primitive mentality, which was to be his sole occupation till his death in 1939. Though his fundamental assumptions are sociological, and he could therefore be classed with those writers I have been speaking about, he does not fit too easily into their category, and he always refused to identify himself with the Durkheimian group; so it is only in a formal sense that he can be called, as Webb calls him, one of Durkheim's collaborators.[1] He remained more of the philosopher pure and simple; hence his interest in primitive systems of thought rather than in primitive institutions. He held that one might as legitimately begin a study of social life by analysis of ways of thought as of ways of behaviour. Perhaps one should say

[1] C. C. J. Webb, *Group Theories of Religion and the Individual*, 1916, pp. 13 and 41.

that he studied them primarily as a logician, for the question of logic is a crucial one in his books, as indeed in a study of systems of thought it should be.

His first two books about primitive peoples, translated into English under the titles of *How Natives Think* and *Primitive Mentality*, set forth the general theory of primitive mentality for which he became so well known. His later works were an amplification of it, though he seems in them also to have slowly modified his original views in the light of modern field reports, for he was a modest and humble man. At the end of his life he may have reversed his position, or at any rate considered doing so, if one may judge from his posthumous *Carnets*. Nevertheless, it was his views as set forth in the earlier books which constituted his distinctive theoretical contribution to anthropology, and it is therefore these I must discuss.

Like Durkheim, he condemns the English School for trying to explain social facts by processes of individual thought— their own—which are the product of different conditions from those which have moulded the minds they seek to understand. They think out how they would have reached beliefs and practices of primitive peoples, and then assume that these peoples must have reached them by those steps. In any case, it is useless to try to interpret primitive minds in terms of individual psychology. The mentality of the individual is derived from the collective representations of his society, which are obligatory for him; and these representations are functions of institutions. Consequently, certain types of representations, and therefore certain ways of thinking, belong to certain types of social structure. In other words, as social structures vary, so will the representations, and consequently the individual's thinking. Every type of society has therefore its distinctive mentality, for each has its distinctive customs and institutions, which are fundamentally only a certain aspect of collective representations; they are, so to speak, the representations considered objectively. Lévy-Bruhl did not mean by this that the representations of a people are any less real than their institutions.

Now, one can classify human societies into a number of different types, but, says Lévy-Bruhl, considered in the

broadest possible way, there are two major types, the primitive and the civilized, and there are two and opposed types of
thought corresponding to them, so we may speak of primitive
mentality and civilized mentality, for they are different not
merely in degree, but in quality. It will be observed that he
wishes to emphasize the differences between civilized and
primitive peoples; this is perhaps the most important single
observation to be made about his theoretical standpoint,
and is what gives it much of its originality. For various
reasons most writers about primitive peoples had tended to
lay stress on the similarities, or what they supposed to be the
similarities, between ourselves and them; and Lévy-Bruhl
thought it might be as well, for a change, to draw attention
to the differences. The criticism often brought against him,
that he did not perceive how very like primitives we are in
many respects, loses much of its force, once we recognize his
intention: he wanted to stress the differences, and in order
to bring them out more clearly, he spotlighted them and
left the similarities in shadow. He knew that he was making
a distortion—what some people like to call an ideal construct
—but he never pretended to be doing anything else, and his
procedure is methodologically justifiable.

We in Europe, says Lévy-Bruhl, have behind us many
centuries of rigorous intellectual speculation and analysis.
Consequently, we are logically orientated, in the sense that
we normally seek the causes of phenomena in natural processes; and even when we face a phenomenon which we cannot account for scientifically, we take it for granted that this is
only because our knowledge is insufficient. Primitive thought
has an altogether different character. It is orientated towards
the supernatural.

The attitude of the mind of the primitive is very different. The
nature of the milieu in which he lives presents itself to him in
quite a different way. Objects and beings are all involved in a
network of mystical participations and exclusions. It is these
which constitute its texture and order. It is then these which
immediately impose themselves on his attention and which alone
retain it. If a phenomenon interests him, if he is not content to
perceive it, so to speak, passively and without reaction, he will

think at once, as by a sort of mental reflex, of an occult and invisible power of which the phenomenon is a manifestation.[1]

And if it be asked why primitive peoples do not inquire, as
we do, into objective causal connexions, the answer is that
they are prevented from doing so by their collective representations, which are prelogical and mystical.

These assertions were rejected out of hand by British anthropologists, whose empirical tradition made them distrust
anything in the nature of philosophical speculation. Lévy-
Bruhl was a mere armchair theorist who, like the rest of his
French colleagues, had never seen a primitive man, far less
talked to one. I think I may claim to be one of the few
anthropologists here or in America who spoke up for him,
not because I agreed with him, but because I felt that a
scholar should be criticized for what he has said, and not
for what he is supposed to have said. My defence had
therefore to be exegetical,[2] an attempt to explain what Lévy-
Bruhl meant by his key expressions and concepts which
evoked so much hostility: prelogical, mentality, collective
representations, mystical, and participations. This terminology makes, at any rate for a British reader, his thought
obscure, so that one is often in doubt what he wished
to say.

Lévy-Bruhl calls 'prelogical' those modes of thought
(magico-religious thought, he did not distinguish between
magic and religion) which appear so true to primitive man
and so absurd to the European. He means by this word
something quite different from what his critics said he meant
by it. He does not mean that primitives are incapable of
thinking coherently, but merely that most of their beliefs
are incompatible with a critical and scientific view of the
universe. They also contain evident contradictions. He is
not saying that primitives are unintelligent, but that their
beliefs are unintelligible to us. This does not mean that we
cannot follow their reasoning. We can, for they reason quite

[1] L. Lévy-Bruhl, *La Mentalité primitive*, 14th edit. (1947), pp. 17–18.
[2] E. E. Evans-Pritchard, 'Lévy-Bruhl's Theory of Primitive Mentality',
Bulletin of the Faculty of Arts, Egyptian University (Cairo), 1934.

logically; but they start from different premisses, and premisses which are to us absurd. They are reasonable, but
they reason in categories different from ours. They are logical,
but the principles of their logic are not ours, not those of
Aristotelian logic. Lévy-Bruhl does not hold that 'logical
principles are foreign to the minds of primitives; a conception of which the absurdity is evident the moment it is formulated. Prelogical does not mean alogical or anti-logical.
Prelogical, applied to primitive mentality, means simply that
it does not go out of its way, as we do, to avoid contradiction.
It does not have always present the same logical require-
ments. What to our eyes is impossible or absurd it often
accepts without seeing any difficulty involved.'[1] Here Lévy-
Bruhl was being too subtle, for he means by 'prelogical'
little more than unscientific or uncritical, that primitive man
is rational but unscientific or uncritical.

When he says that 'primitive mentality' or the 'primitive
mind' is prelogical, hopelessly uncritical, he is not speaking
of an individual's ability, or inability, to reason, but of the
categories in which he reasons. He is speaking, not of a
biological or psychological difference between primitives and
ourselves, but of a social one. It follows, therefore, that he is
also not speaking of a type of mind such as some psychologists and others have delineated: intuitive, logical, romantic,
classical, and so on. What he is speaking about are axioms,
values, and sentiments—more or less what are sometimes
called patterns of thought—and he says that among primitive peoples these tend to be mystical and therefore beyond
verification, impervious to experience, and indifferent to
contradiction. Taking the same stand as Durkheim on this
issue, he declares that they are social, not psychological, facts,
and like all such are general, traditional, and obligatory.
They are present before the individual who acquires them
is born and they will be present after he is dead. Even the
affective states which accompany the ideas are socially
determined. In this sense, therefore, a people's mentality
is something objective. If it were simply an individual

---

[1] Lévy-Bruhl, *La Mentalité primitive* (The Herbert Spencer Lecture), 1931,
p. 21.

phenomenon, it would be a subjective one; its generality makes it an objective one.

These modes or patterns of thought which in their totality make up the mind or mentality of a people are what Lévy-Bruhl calls collective representations, an expression in common use among French sociologists of the time, and a translation, I think, of the German *Vorstellung*. It suggests something very abstruse, whereas he means by it little more than what we call an idea, or a notion, or a belief; and when he says that a representation is collective, he means no more than that it is common to all, or most, members of a society. Every society has its collective representations. Ours tend always to be critical and scientific, those of primitive peoples to be mystical. Lévy-Bruhl would, I think, have agreed that for most people both alike are fiduciary.

If Lévy-Bruhl had wished to arouse an Englishman's worst suspicions, he could not have done better than he did by the use of the word 'mystical'. Yet he makes it clear that he means no more by this term than what English writers mean when they speak of belief in the supernatural—of magic and religion and so forth. He says 'I employ this term, for lack of a better, not with allusion to the religious mysticism of our own societies, which is something altogether different, but in the strictly defined sense where "mystical" is used for the belief in forces, in influences, and in actions imperceptible to the senses, though none the less real.'[1] Now, the collective representations of primitive peoples are pre-eminently concerned with these imperceptible forces. Consequently, as soon as primitive man's sensations become conscious perceptions, they are coloured by the mystical ideas they evoke. They are immediately conceptualized in a mystical category of thought. The concept dominates the sensation, and imposes its image on it. One might say that primitive man sees an object as we see it, but he perceives it differently, for as soon as he gives conscious attention to it, the mystical idea of the object comes between him and the object, and transforms its purely objective properties. We also perceive

---

[1] Lévy-Bruhl, *Les Fonctions mentales dans les sociétés inférieures*, 2nd edit. (1912), p. 30.

in the object the collective representation of our culture, but since that accords with its objective features, we perceive it objectively. The primitive man's collective representation of it is mystical, and consequently he perceives it mystically and in a manner entirely foreign, and indeed absurd, to us. The mystical perception is immediate. Primitive man does not, for example, perceive a shadow and apply to it the doctrine of his society, according to which it is one of his souls. When he is conscious of his shadow he is aware of his soul. We can best understand Lévy-Bruhl's view if we say that, in his way of looking at the matter, beliefs only arise late in the development of human thought, when perception and representation have already fallen apart. We can then say that a person perceives his shadow and believes it to be his soul. The question of belief does not arise among primitive peoples. The belief is contained in the shadow. The shadow is the belief. In the same way, a primitive man does not perceive a leopard and believe that it is his totem-brother. What he perceives is his totem-brother. The physical qualities of a leopard are fused in the mystical representation of totem, and are subordinated to it. 'The reality', says Lévy-Bruhl, 'in which primitives move is itself mystical. Not a being, not an object, not a natural phenomenon in their collective representations is what it appears to us. Almost all that we see in it escapes them, or they are indifferent to it. On the other hand, they see in it many things which we do not even suspect.'[1]

He goes even further than this. He says not merely that the perceptions of primitives embody mystical representations, but that it is the mystical representations which evoke the perceptions. In the stream of sensory impressions, only a few become conscious ones. Men only notice or pay attention to a little of what they see and hear. What they pay attention to is selected on account of its greater affectivity. In other words, a man's interests are the selective agents, and these are to a great extent socially determined. Primitives pay attention to phenomena on account of the mystical properties their collective representations have endowed them with.

[1] *Les Fonctions mentales*, pp. 30–31.

The collective representations thus both control perception and are fused with it. Primitive peoples pay great attention to their shadows precisely because, in their representations, their shadows are their souls. We do not do so, because a shadow is nothing positive for us, just a negation of light; and their and our representations in this matter are mutually exclusive. So, it is not so much that perception of a shadow causes the belief (that what is perceived is the soul) to enter into consciousness, but rather the belief that causes primitive man to pay attention to his shadow. Collective representations, by the value they give to phenomena, direct attention to them, and since representations differ widely between rude and civilized peoples, what they notice in the world around them will be different, or at least the reasons for their paying attention to phenomena will be different.

The representations of primitive peoples have a quality of their own, namely the quality of being mystical, which is quite foreign to our own representations, and therefore we may speak of primitive mentality as something *sui generis*. The logical principle of these mystical representations is what Lévy-Bruhl calls the law of mystical participation. The collective representations of primitive peoples consist of a network of participations which, since the representations are mystical, are mystical also. In primitive thought, things are connected so that what affects one is believed to affect others, not objectively but by mystical action (though primitive man himself does not distinguish between objective and mystical action). Primitive peoples, indeed, are often more concerned about what we would call the supra-sensible or, to use Lévy-Bruhl's term, mystical, relations between things than about what we would call the objective relations between them. To take the example I have used before, some primitive peoples participate in their shadows, so what affects their shadows affects them. Hence it would be fatal for a man to cross an open space at midday, because he would lose his shadow. Other primitive peoples participate in their names, and they will therefore not reveal them, for were an enemy to learn a name, he would have the owner of it also in his power. Among other peoples, a man participates in his

child, so when the child is sick he, and not the child, drinks
the medicine. These participations form the structure of
categories in which primitive man moves and out of which his
social personality is built. There are mystical participations
between a man and the land on which he dwells, between a
man and his chief, a man and his kin, a man and his totem,
and so on, covering every side of his life.

It may here be noted that, while Lévy-Bruhl's participations resemble the associations of ideas of Tylor and Frazer,
the conclusions he draws from them are very different to
theirs. For Tylor and Frazer primitive man believes in magic
because he reasons incorrectly from his observations. For
Lévy-Bruhl he reasons incorrectly because his reasoning is
determined by the mystical representations of his society.
The first is an explanation in terms of individual psychology,
the second a sociological explanation. Lévy-Bruhl is certainly correct in so far as any given individual is concerned,
for the individual learns the patterns of thought in which,
and by which, mystical connexions are established. He does
not deduce them from his own observations.

Lévy-Bruhl's discussion of the law of mystical participation is perhaps the most valuable, as well as being a highly
original, part of his thesis. He was one of the first, if not the
first, to emphasize that primitive ideas, which seem so strange
to us, and indeed sometimes idiotic, when considered as
isolated facts, are meaningful when seen as parts of patterns
of ideas and behaviour, each part having an intelligible
relationship to the others. He recognized that values form
systems as coherent as the logical constructions of the intellect,
that there is a logic of sentiments as well as of reason, though
based on a different principle. His analysis is not like the
just-so stories we have earlier considered, for he does not try
to explain primitive magic and religion by a theory purporting to show how they might have come about, what is their
cause or origin. He takes them as given, and seeks only to show
their structure and the way in which they are evidence of a
distinctive mentality common to all societies of a certain type.

In order to emphasize the distinctiveness of this mentality,
he made out that primitive thought in general differs alto-

gether, in quality and not just in degree, from our own (even though there may be people in our own society who think and feel like primitives, and in every person there may be a substratum of primitive mentality), and this, his main theme, cannot be sustained; and at the end of his life he himself appears to have abandoned it. If it were true, we would scarcely be able to communicate with primitives, even to learn their languages. The single fact that we can do so shows that Lévy-Bruhl was making too strong a contrast between the primitive and the civilized. His error was partly due to the poverty of the material at his disposal when he first formulated his theory, and to the double selection, to which I have earlier referred, of the curious and the sensational at the expense of the mundane and matter-of-fact. Then, when Lévy-Bruhl contrasts us with primitives, who are we, and who are the primitives? He does not distinguish between the different sorts of us, the different social and occupational strata of our society, more pronounced fifty years ago than today; nor between us at different periods of our history. In his sense of the word, did the philosophers of the Sorbonne and the Breton peasantry, or the fishermen of Normandy, have the same mentality? And, since the modern European developed from barbarism, from a type of society characterized by primitive mentality, how and when did our ancestors pass from the one to the other? Such a development could not have taken place at all unless our primitive forebears, side by side with their mystical notions, had also a body of empirical knowledge to guide them; and Lévy-Bruhl has to accept that savages sometimes wake from their dreams, that it is necessary in the performance of their technical activities that 'the representations coincide in some essential points with objective reality, and that the practices are, at a certain moment, effectively adapted to the ends pursued'.[1] But he does so only as a minor concession, and without prejudice to his position. Yet it is self-evident that, far from being such children of fancy as he makes them out to be, they have less chance to be than we, for they live closer to the harsh realities of nature, which permit survival

---

[1] *Les Fonctions mentales*, pp. 354–5.

only to those who are guided in their pursuits by observation, experiment, and reason.

One might further inquire into which class Plato falls, or the symbolic thought of Philo and Plotinus; and all the more so in that, among his examples of primitive mentality, we find such peoples as the Chinese included with Polynesians, Melanesians, Negroes, American Indians, and Australian Blackfellows. It must also be remarked once again that, as in so many anthropological theories, negative instances are ignored. For example, many primitive peoples do not at all bother about their shadows or their names, yet typologically, on his own classification, they belong to the same class of societies as those who do.

There is no reputable anthropologist who today accepts this theory of two distinct types of mentality. All observers who have made lengthy first-hand studies of primitive peoples are agreed that they are for the most part interested in practical affairs, which they conduct in an empirical manner, either without the least reference to supra-sensible forces, influences, and actions, or in a way in which these have a subordinate and auxiliary role. It may be noted also that what Lévy-Bruhl defines as the most fundamental feature of primitive, or prelogical, mentality, its failure to perceive, or its lack of concern at, evident contradictions, is very largely illusory. He is perhaps not entirely to blame for not seeing it to be such, for the results of intensive modern field research had not been published when he wrote his best-known works. He could not then, I think, have realized that, at any rate to a large degree, the contradictions only appear to be glaring when the European observer sets down side by side beliefs which in reality are found in different situations and at different levels of experience. Nor perhaps could he have appreciated, as well as we can today, that mystical representations are not necessarily aroused by objects outside their use in ritual situations, that they are not, as it were, inevitably evoked by the objects. For example, some peoples put stones in the forks of trees to delay the setting of the sun; but the stone so used is casually picked up, and has only a mystical significance in, and for the purpose and duration of, the rite. The sight of this or any other stone in any other situation does not evoke the idea of the setting sun. The association, as I pointed out in discussing Frazer, is brought about by the rite, and need not in other situations arise. It may be observed also that objects such as fetishes and idols are humanly constructed, and in their material selves have no significance; they only acquire that when they are endowed with supernatural power through a rite which, also by human agency, infuses in them that power, object and its virtue thus being separated in the mind. Then again, in childhood, mystical notions cannot be evoked by objects which for adults have mystical significance, for the child does not yet know them; and he may not even notice the objects— a child, at least very often with us, one day discovers his shadow. Moreover, objects which have mystical value for some people have none at all for others—a totem sacred to one clan is eaten by members of other clans in the same community. Such considerations suggest that a more subtle interpretation is required. Again, I believe that at the time he wrote he could not have made, as we can make today, due allowance for the vast complexity and rich symbolism of primitive languages and of the thought they express. What appear to be hopeless contradictions when translated into English may not appear so in the native language. When, for instance, a native statement is translated that a man of such-and-such a clan is a leopard, it appears to us to be absurd, but the word he uses which we translate by 'is' may not have the same meaning for him that the word 'is' has for us. In any case, there is no inherent contradiction in saying that a man is a leopard. The leopard quality is something added in thought to the human attributes, and does not detract from them. Things may be thought of in different ways in different contexts. In one sense it is one thing, and in another sense it is something more than that thing.

Lévy-Bruhl is also wrong in supposing that there is necessarily a contradiction between an objective causal explanation and a mystical one. It is not so. The two kinds of explanation can be, as indeed they are, held together, the one supplementing the other; and they are not therefore exclusive. For example, the dogma that death is due to witchcraft does not exclude the observation that the man was killed by a buffalo. For Lévy-Bruhl there is here a contradiction, to which natives are indifferent. But no contradiction is involved. On the contrary, the natives are making a very acute analysis of the situation. They are perfectly well aware that a buffalo killed the man, but they hold that he would not have been killed by it if he had not been bewitched. Why otherwise should he have been killed by it, why he and not someone else, why by that buffalo and not by another, why at that time and place and not at another? They are asking why, as we would put it, two independent chains of events crossed each other, bringing a certain man and a certain buffalo into a single point of time and space. You will agree that there is no contradiction here, but that on the contrary the witch-craft explanation supplements that of natural causation, accounting for what we would call the element of chance. The witchcraft cause of the accident is emphasized because, of the two causes, only the mystical one permits intervention, vengeance on a witch. The same mixture of empirical knowledge and mystical notions may be found in primitive ideas about procreation, drugs, and other matters. The objective properties of things and natural causation of events may be known, but are not socially emphasized or are denied because they conflict with some social dogma which is in accordance with some institution, mystical belief being in these circumstances more appropriate than empirical knowledge. Indeed, we may again assert that if this were not so it would be difficult to see how scientific thought could ever have emerged. Moreover, a social representation is not acceptable if it conflicts with individual experience, unless the conflict can be accounted for in terms of the representa-tion itself or of some other representation, the explanation then being, however, acknowledgement of the conflict. A representation which asserts that fire does not burn the hand thrust into it would not long survive. A representation which asserts that it will not burn you if you have sufficient faith may survive. Indeed, Lévy-Bruhl, as we have seen, admits that mystical thought is conditioned by experience, that in activities such as war, hunting, fishing, treatment of ailments, and divination means must be rationally adapted to ends.

Lévy-Bruhl, it is now, I think, unanimously agreed among anthropologists, made primitive peoples far more superstitious, to use a commoner word than prelogical, than they really are; and he made the contrast more glaring between their mentality and ours by presenting us as more positivistic than most of us are. From my talks with him I would say that in this matter he felt himself in a quandary. For him, Christianity and Judaism were also superstitions, indicative of prelogical and mystical mentality, and on his definitions necessarily so. But, I think in order not to cause offence, he made no allusion to them. So he excluded the mystical in our own culture as rigorously as he excluded the empirical in savage cultures. This failure to take into account the beliefs and rites of the vast majority of his fellow countrymen vitiates his argument. And he himself, as Bergson naughtily observed, in constantly accusing primitive man of not attributing any event to chance, accepted chance. He thereby placed himself, on his own showing, in the prelogical class.

However, this does not mean that, in his sense of the word, primitive thought is not more 'mystical' than ours. The contrast Lévy-Bruhl makes is an exaggeration, but, all the same, primitive magic and religion confront us with a real problem, and not one imagined by the French philosopher. Men with long experience of primitive peoples have felt confounded by it; and it is true that primitives often, and especially in misfortunes, attribute events to supra-sensible forces where we, with our greater knowledge, account for them by natural causation, or seek to do so. But, even so, I think that Lévy-Bruhl could have posed the problem to better advantage. It is not so much a question of primitive versus civilized mentality as the relation of two types of thought to each other in any society, whether primitive or civilized, a problem of levels of thought and experience. It was because Lévy-Bruhl was dominated, as were almost all writers of the period, by notions of evolution and inevitable progress that he did not appreciate this. Had he not been so positivistic in his own representations, he might have asked himself, not what are the differences between civilized and primitive modes of thought, but what are the functions of the two kinds of thought in any society, or in human society in general—the kinds associated with what are sometimes distinguished as the 'expressive' and the 'instrumental'.[1] The problem would then have appeared to him in a rather different light, as it appeared in various forms to Pareto, Bergson, William James, Max Weber, and others. I can best present it in a preliminary way by a brief discussion of what Pareto says of civilized thought, for his treatise forms an ironical commentary on Lévy-Bruhl's thesis. Lévy-Bruhl says of the mentality of our society 'I consider it as well enough defined by the works of philosophers, logicians, and psychologists, ancient and modern, without prejudging what a later sociological analysis may modify in the conclusions reached by them up to now.'[2] Pareto draws on European writings, by philosophers and others, to prove that the mentality of Europeans is very largely irrational, or, as he calls it, non-logico-experimental.

In Vilfredo Pareto's vast *Trattato di sociologia generale*, translated into English under the title of *The Mind and Society*, over a million words are devoted to an analysis of feelings and ideas. I am only going to speak of that part of his treatise which has some relevance to the subject of primitive mentality. He, also, uses a peculiar terminology. There are in any society 'residues'—for convenience we may call them sentiments—some of which make for social stability, and others for social change. Sentiments are expressed in behaviour and also in 'derivations' (what other writers call ideologies or rationalizations). Now, most actions, in which term Pareto includes thought, which express these residues or sentiments are non-logico-experimental (non-logical, for short), and they must be distinguished from logico-experimental (for short, logical) actions. Logical thought depends on facts and not the facts on it, whereas non-logical thought

---

[1] See J. Beattie for a recent discussion of this distinction in *Other Cultures*, 1964, chap. xii.
[2] *Les Fonctions mentales*, p. 21.

is accepted *a priori*, and dictates to experience; and should it conflict with experience, arguments are evoked to re-establish accord. Logical actions (and thought) are connected with arts, sciences, and economics, and are also exemplified in military, legal, and political operations. In other social processes non-logical actions (and thought) predominate. The test of whether actions are logical or non-logical is whether their subjective purpose accords with their objective results, whether means are objectively adapted to ends; and the sole judge of this test must be modern science, that is, the factual knowledge we ourselves at any time possess.

By 'non-logical' Pareto does not mean, any more than Lévy-Bruhl meant by prelogical, that thought and action so classed are illogical, but simply that they only subjectively, and not objectively, conjoin means to ends. Nor must we confuse the issue with that of utility. An objectively valid belief may not have utility for the society or for the individual who holds it, whereas a doctrine which is absurd from a logico-experimental standpoint may be beneficial to both. Indeed, Pareto states it as his aim to demonstrate experimentally 'the individual and social utility of non-logical conduct'.[1] (The same point has, of course, often been made, by Frazer, for example, who tells us that at a certain level of culture government, private property, marriage, and respect for human life 'have derived much of their strength from beliefs which nowadays we should condemn unreservedly as superstitious and absurd'.[2])

Moreover, the search for causes, however imaginary those found may turn out to be, has led to the discovery of real ones eventually: 'if one were to assert that but for theology and metaphysics experimental science would not even exist, one could not be easily confuted. Those three kinds of activity are probably manifestations of one same psychic state, on the extinction of which they would vanish simultaneously.'[3]

[1] V. Pareto, *The Mind and Society*, 1935, p. 35. See also his *Le Mythe vertuiste et la littérature immorale*, 1911.
[2] Frazer, *Psyche's Task*, 1913, p. 4.
[3] Pareto, *The Mind and Society*, p. 591.

But all the same, how does it come about that people capable of logical behaviour so often act in a non-logical manner? Tylor and Frazer say it is because they reason erroneously; Marett, Malinoswki, and Freud say it is to relieve tensions; Lévy-Bruhl, and in a sense Durkheim, say it is because collective representations direct their thought. Pareto says it is on account of their residues. I have substituted for this word 'sentiments', and Pareto himself often uses the words interchangeably; but strictly speaking, Pareto's residues are the common elements in forms of thought and action, uniformities abstracted from observed behaviour and speech, and sentiments are conceptualizations of these abstractions, constant attitudes which, though we cannot observe them, we may assume to exist from the constant elements observed in behaviour. Thus, a residue is an abstraction from observed behaviour, and a sentiment is a higher level of abstraction—an hypothesis. An example may help here. Men have always feasted, but many different reasons have been given for their banquets. 'Banquets in honour of the dead become banquets in honour of the gods, and then again banquets in honour of saints; and then finally they go back and become merely commemorative banquets again. Forms can be changed, but it is much more difficult to suppress the banquets.'[1] In Pareto's language, the banquet is the residue and the reason for holding it is the derivation. It is no special sort of banquet, but simply the act of banqueting in all times and in all places, which constitutes the residue. The constant attitude which lies behind this constant element in banqueting is what Pareto calls a sentiment. Nevertheless, so long as we know we are writing shorthand, sentiment may be used for both the abstraction and the conceptualization of it. Also, strictly speaking, Pareto's derivations are the inconstant elements in action, but as these are so often the reasons given for doing something, in contrast to the constant element, the doing of it, Pareto generally uses the word to denote the reasons people give for their behaviour. Sentiment is thus expressed both in action and in the rationalization of it, because men have not only need for

[1] *The Mind and Society*, p. 607.

action but also need to intellectualize it, to justify themselves for performing it, whether by sound or absurd arguments matters little. Residue and derivation are thus both derived from sentiment, but the derivation is secondary and the less important. It is therefore useless to interpret behaviour by the reason men give to explain it. On this point Pareto severely criticized Herbert Spencer and Tylor, for deriving cults of the dead from the reasons given, namely that souls and ghosts exist. We should rather say that the cults give rise to the reasons, which are only rationalizations of what is done. He likewise criticized Fustel de Coulanges for saying that ownership of land arose as a consequence of a religious idea, the belief that the ancestral ghosts lived in the ground, whereas ownership of land and religion are likely to have developed side by side, the relationship between religion and ownership of land being one of reciprocal interdependence and not a simple, one-way, cause-and-effect one. But though ideologies may react on sentiments, it is the sentiments, or perhaps we should here say the residues, the constant modes of behaviour, which are basic and durable, and the ideas, the derivations, are, as it were, merely an attachment, and a variable and inconstant one. Ideologies change, but the sentiments which give rise to them remain unchanged. The same residue may even give rise to opposed derivations: for example, what Pareto calls the sex residue may be expressed in violent hatred of all sexual manifestations. The derivations are always dependent on the residues, and not the residues on them. People give all sorts of reasons for dispensing hospitality, but all insist on the hospitality. The giving of it is the residue, the reasons for giving it are the derivations, and they matter little, almost any reason serving the purpose equally well. So, if you can convince a man that his reasons for doing something are erroneous, he will not stop doing it, but will find some other reasons to justify his conduct. Here Pareto, rather unexpectedly, quotes Herbert Spencer approvingly when he says that not ideas but feelings, to which ideas serve only as a guide, govern the world, or perhaps we should say feelings expressed in action, in the residues.

Logically [Pareto wrote], one ought first to believe in a given religion and then in the efficacy of its rites, the efficacy, logically, being the consequence of the belief. Logically, it is absurd to offer a prayer unless there is someone to hearken to it. But non-logical conduct is derived by a precisely reverse process. There is first an instinctive belief in the efficacy of a rite, then an 'explanation' of the belief is desired, then it is found in religion.[1]

There are certain elementary types of behaviour, found in all societies in similar situations and directed towards similar objects. These, the residues, are relatively constant, since they spring from strong sentiments. The exact manner in which the sentiments are expressed, and in particular the ideologies which accompany their expression, are variable. Men in each society express them in the particular idiom of their culture. Their interpretations 'assume the forms that are most generally prevalent in the ages in which they are evolved. These are comparable to the styles of costume worn by people in the periods corresponding.'[2] If we want to understand human beings, therefore, we must always get behind their ideas and study their behaviour; and once we recognize that sentiments control behaviour, it is not difficult for us to understand the actions of men of remote times, because residues change little through centuries, even millennia. If this were not so, how could we still enjoy the poems of Homer and the elegies, tragedies, and comedies of the Greeks and Romans? They express sentiments in which, in great part at least, we share. Social forms remain, says Pareto, fundamentally the same; only the cultural idiom in which they are expressed changes. Pareto's conclusion maybe summarized in the dictum 'human nature does not change', or, in his own words, 'derivations vary, the residue endures'.[3] Pareto thus agrees with those who hold that in the beginning was the deed.

Pareto, like Crawley, Frazer, Lévy-Bruhl, and others of their period, was a scissors-and-paste writer, taking his examples from here, there, and everywhere, and fitting them into a rather elementary classification; and his judgements

---

[1] *The Mind and Society*, p. 569.   [2] Ibid., p. 143.
[3] Ibid., p. 660.

are shallow. Nevertheless, his treatise is of interest to us because, although he does not discuss primitive peoples in it, it has some relevance to Lévy-Bruhl's presentation of their mentality. Lévy-Bruhl tells us that primitives are prelogical in contrast to us, who are logical. Pareto tells us that we are, for the most part, non-logical. Theology, metaphysics, socialism, parliaments, democracy, universal suffrage, republics, progress, and what have you, are quite as irrational as anything primitives believe in, in that they are the product of faith and sentiment, and not of experiment and reasoning. And the same may be said of most of our ideas and actions: our morals, our loyalties to our families and countries, and so forth. In his volumes Pareto gives logical notions and behaviour in European societies about as much space as Lévy-Bruhl gives them in primitive societies. We may be a little more critical and sensible than we used to be, but not so much as to make a big difference. The relative areas of the logico-experimental and the non-logico-experimental are fairly constant throughout history and in all societies.

But, though Pareto's conclusions are thus contradictory to those of Lévy-Bruhl, some resemblance between the analytical concepts they employ may be noted. 'Non-logico-experimental' corresponds to 'prelogical', 'residues' correspond to 'mystical participations'; for, for Pareto, residues are abstractions of relational elements common to all societies when variable accretions have been removed, such as relations with family and kin, places, the dead, and so forth. Particular participations—of a man in his country's flag, in his church, in his school, in his regiment, the network of sentiments in which modern man lives—would be, for Pareto, derivations. And, in general, we may say that his 'derivations' correspond to Lévy-Bruhl's 'collective representations'. Also, both wanted to make the same point, that, outside empirical or scientific behaviour, people aim at ensuring that their notions and conduct shall be in accord with sentiments and values, and they do not worry whether their premises are scientifically valid or their inferences entirely logical; and these sentiments and values form a system of thought with a logic of its own. Any occurrence is at once interpreted, as Lévy-Bruhl puts it, in terms of collective representations, and as Pareto puts it, in terms of derivations—in the logic of representations or of sentiments which underlie the derivations. It is they, and not science, which set the standard for living. It is only, as Pareto sees it, in the technological field that science has gained ground from sentiment in modern society. Hence our difficulty in understanding primitive magic and witchcraft, while we readily understand most of the other notions of primitive peoples, since they accord with sentiments we ourselves have. Sentiments are superior to bare observation and experiment, and they dictate to them in ordinary everyday life.

The main theoretical differences between the two authors are that Lévy-Bruhl regarded mystical thought and behaviour as socially determined, while Pareto regarded it as psychologically determined; that Lévy-Bruhl tended to see behaviour as a product of thought, of representations, while Pareto treated thought, derivations, as secondary and unimportant; and that, while Lévy-Bruhl opposed primitive mentality to civilized mentality, in Pareto's view basic sentiments are constant, and do not vary, or at least not greatly, with types of social structure. It is the last difference that I wish particularly to stress, for, in spite of his superficiality and vulgarity and the confusion of his thoughts, Pareto saw the problem correctly. In an address delivered in Lausanne, he said:

Human activity has two main branches: that of sentiment and that of experimental research. One cannot exaggerate the importance of the first. It is sentiment which impels to action, which gives life to moral rules, to duty, and to religions, under all their so complex and so various forms. It is by aspiration to the ideal that human societies subsist and progress. But the second branch is also essential for these societies; it provides the material which the first makes use of; we owe to it the knowledge which makes for efficacious action and useful modification of sentiment, thanks to which it adapts itself little by little, very slowly, it is true, to prevailing circumstances. All the sciences, the natural as well as the social, have been in their beginnings, a mixture of sentiment and experiment. Centuries have been necessary to bring about a separation of these elements, which, in our time, is almost entirely accomplished for the natural sciences and which has begun and continues for the social sciences.[1]

It was his intention to study the part played by logical and non-logical thought and action in the same type of culture and society, Europe ancient and modern, but he did not carry it out. He wrote at enormous length about what he regarded as fallacious beliefs and irrational behaviour, but he tells us very little about common sense and scientific beliefs and empirical behaviour. So, just as Lévy-Bruhl leaves us with the impression of primitives who are almost continuously engaged in ritual and under the dominance of mystical beliefs, Pareto leaves us with the impression of Europeans at all periods of their history at the mercy of sentiments, expressed in a vast variety of what he considers to be absurd notions and actions.

[1] Address. *Journal d'Économie Politique*, 1917, pp. 426 ff. Appendix to G. C. Homans and C. P. Curtis, *An Introduction to Pareto. His Sociology*, 1934.

V

CONCLUSION

I HAVE given you an account, with some illustrations, of various types of theory which have been put forward to explain the religious beliefs and practices of primitive man. For the most part the theories we have been discussing are, for anthropologists at least, as dead as mutton, and to-day are chiefly of interest as specimens of the thought of their time. Some of the books—those, for example, of Tylor, Frazer, and Durkheim—will doubtless continue to be read as classics, but they are no longer much of a stimulus for the student. Others—for example, Lang, King, Crawley, and Marett—have more or less passed into oblivion. That these theories no longer make much appeal is due to a number of factors, a few of which I shall mention.

One reason is, I believe, that religion has ceased to occupy men's minds in the way it did at the end of last, and at the beginning of this, century. Anthropological writers then felt that they were living at a momentous crisis in the history of thought, and that they had their part to play in it. Max Müller remarked in 1878 that 'Every day, every week, every month, every quarter, the most widely read journals seem just now to vie with each other in telling us that the time for religion is past, that faith is a hallucination or an infantile disease, that the gods have at last been found out and exploded . . . .'[1] Crawley wrote, twenty-seven years later, in 1905, that the enemies of religion 'have developed the opposition of science and religion into a deadly struggle, and the opinion is everywhere gaining ground that religion is a mere survival from a primitive and mythopoeic age, and its extinction only a matter of time'.[2] I have discussed elsewhere[3]

[1] *Lectures on the Origin and Growth of Religion*, 1878, p. 218.

[2] Crawley, *The Tree of Life*, 1905, p. 8.

[3] Evans-Pritchard, 'Religion and the Anthropologists', *Blackfriars*, Apr. 1960, pp. 104–18.

35.2.28

the part played by anthropologists in this struggle, so I do not pursue the matter any further. I mention it here only because I think that the crisis of conscience to some extent accounts for the efflorescence of books on primitive religion during this period, and also that the passing of the crisis may account in some degree for the absence among later generations of anthropologists of the passionate interest their predecessors had in the subject. The last book in which one senses a feeling of urgency and conflict is S. A. Cook's *The Study of Religion*, finished and published when the calamity of 1914 had already fallen.

There were other reasons why the debate abated. Anthropology was becoming an experimental subject, and as field research developed, both in quality and in quantity, what appeared to be more in the nature of philosophical speculation on the part of scholars who had never seen a primitive people was at a discount. It was not merely that facts revealed by modern research only too often cast doubt on earlier theories, but that the theories came to be seen to have faulty construction. When anthropologists attempted to make use of them in their field studies, they found that they had little experimental value, because they were formulated in terms which seldom permitted their being broken down into problems which observation could solve, so they could not be proved either true or false. What use as a guide to field research are Tylor's and Müller's and Durkheim's theories of the genesis of religion?

It is the word genesis on which emphasis is placed. It was because explanations of religion were offered in terms of origins that these theoretical debates, once so full of life and fire, eventually subsided. To my mind, it is extraordinary that anyone could have thought it worth while to speculate about what might have been the origin of some custom or belief, when there is absolutely no means of discovering, in the absence of historical evidence, what was its origin. And yet this is what almost all our authors explicitly or implicitly did, whether their theses were psychological or sociological; even those most hostile to what they dubbed pseudo-history were not immune from putting forward similar explanations themselves. A long essay might be written about the appalling confusion in these discussions with regard to the ideas of evolution, development, history, progress, primitive, origin, genesis, and cause, and I do not propose to unravel it. It must suffice to say that there is little or nothing one can do with such theories.

So many examples have already been given that I cite only one more. Herbert Spencer and Lord Avebury accounted for totemism by a theory which postulated that it originated in the practice of naming individuals, for one reason or another, after animals, plants, and inanimate objects. Let us follow Avebury:[1] these names then became attached to the families of the persons who received them and to their lines of descent; and, when the origin of the names was forgotten, a mysterious relation with the creatures and objects was assumed, and they evoked awe and were worshipped. Apart from the fact that there is no evidence that totemic creatures, at least usually, evoke any response that can legitimately be called awe, and that, in any case, they are not worshipped, how can one possibly know whether totemism originated in this way? It could have done, but how does one set about inquiring into the matter, or testing the validity of the supposition?

Attempts have indeed been made, by German scholars in particular (Ratzel, Frobenius, Gräbner, Ankerman, Foy, Schmidt), whose method was known as the *Kulturkreislehre*, to establish a chronology for primitive cultures from circumstantial evidence. Wilhelm Schmidt was the chief exponent of this method of reconstruction with regard to primitive religions, using such criteria as geographical distribution of hunters and collectors and their low stage of economic development. He considered that peoples who lack the culture of plants and animal husbandry—such peoples as the Pygmies and Pygmoids of Africa and Asia, the aboriginals of south-east Australia, the Andamanese, the Eskimoes, the people of Tierra del Fuego, and some of the American Indians—are the 'ethnologically oldest' peoples. They belong to the primitive culture, which then developed along three

---

[1] *Marriage, Totemism, and Religion. An Answer to Critics*, 1911, pp. 86 ff.

independent and parallel lines: matrilineal and agricultural, patrilineal and totemic, and patriarchal and nomadic, each with its own habit of mind and its own outlook on the world. In the primitive culture there is no totemism, fetish worship, animism, or magic, and ghost worship is found only in a feeble form. On the other hand, these peoples who are lowest in the scale of cultural and social development have, as Andrew Lang had pointed out, a monotheistic religion whose gods are eternal, omniscient, beneficent, moral, omnipotent, and creative, satisfying all man's needs, rational, social, moral, and emotional. Discussions about the priority or otherwise of monotheism go back to pre-anthropological times, e.g. David Hume's *The Natural History of Religion* (1757), in which he pretended (using the word in his eighteenth-century sense) that polytheism or idolatry was the earliest form of religion, basing his case on the facts of history, records about primitive peoples, and logic. The controversies were, as we might expect, coloured by theological considerations and consequently, as in Hume's books and the heat they engendered, tended to be polemical. Hume wrote as a theist, but his religious position might be thought to have been ambiguous. It is above all, as Lang had also surmised, his desire to have a logical cause for the universe which leads man to a belief in God, for this response to a stimulus from without, combined with a tendency towards personification, gives him this idea of a divine person, a supreme being. In respect of this explanation of gods, Lang and Schmidt fall into the class of intellectualist writers. The origin of the conception lies in observation and inference, but, in their view, in this matter both were sound. The theory may be an acceptable hypothesis with regard to creative being, but it does not, it seems to me, explain satisfactorily the prevalence of monotheism among these very simple peoples.

Schmidt wished to discredit the evolutionary ethnologists, according to whose schemata of development these same peoples should be in the lowest grade of fetishism, magism, animism, totemism, and so forth. Undoubtedly he proved his case against them, but only at the cost, as with Lang, of accepting their evolutionary criteria, giving historical chronology to cultural levels. Indeed, on the positive side, I do not think he established his position firmly, and I find his reasoning tendentious and his use of sources dubious. I am much indebted to Pater Schmidt for his exhaustive discussion of the religions of primitives and of theories of primitive religion, but I do not think that his reconstruction of historical levels can be maintained, or that the methods he used can, as he claimed, legitimately be accepted as genuine historical methods. The matter is complicated, and I may be permitted to treat it thus briefly because although Schmidt, a man of forceful personality as well as of great learning, built up for himself a school in Vienna, this school has disintegrated since his death; and I doubt whether today there are many who would defend his chronological reconstructions, which were another attempt to discover the origin of religion where in the circumstances science does not provide us with the means of ascertaining it.

It should, however, be pointed out that true monotheism in the historical sense of the word might be held to be a negation of polytheism, and therefore could not have preceded it; and on this issue I quote Pettazzoni: 'What we find among uncivilized peoples is not monotheism in its historically legitimate sense, but the idea of a Supreme Being, and the erroneous identification, the misleading assimilation, of this idea to true monotheism can give rise only to misunderstandings.'[1]

So we must add monotheism (in Schmidt's sense of the word) to our list of unsupportable hypotheses about its genesis: fetishism, manism, nature-mythism, animism, totemism, dynamism (*mana*, &c.), magism, polytheism, and various psychological states. Nobody, so far as I am aware, defends any of these positions today. The great advances that social anthropology has made in and by field research have turned our eyes away from the vain pursuit of origins, and the many once disputing schools about them have withered away.

I think that most anthropologists would today agree that

[1] Pettazzoni, *Essays on the History of Religions*, p. 9.

it is useless to seek for a *primordium* in religion. Schleiter says, truly, 'all evolutionary schemes of religion, without exception, in the determination of the primordium and the serial stages of alleged development, proceed upon a purely arbitrary and uncontrolled basis'.[1] Also, it has been clearly established that in many primitive religions peoples' minds function in different ways at different levels and in different contexts. So a man may turn to a fetish for certain purposes, and appeal to God in other situations; and a religion can be both polytheistic and monotheistic, according to whether Spirit is thought of as more than one or as one. It is now also clear that even in the same primitive society there may be, as Radin pointed out,[2] wide differences in this respect between individuals, differences he attributes to differences of temperament. Finally, I suppose it would be agreed that the kind of cause-and-effect explanation which was implicit in so much earlier theorizing is hardly in accord with modern scientific thought in general, which seeks rather to reveal and understand constant relations.

In these theories it was assumed, taken for granted, that we were at one end of the scale of human progress and the so-called savages were at the other end, and that, because primitive men were on a rather low technological level, their thought and custom must in all respects be the antithesis of ours. We are rational, primitive peoples prelogical, living in a world of dreams and make-believe, of mystery and awe; we are capitalists, they communists; we are monogamous, they promiscuous; we are monotheists, they fetishists, animists, pre-animists or what have you, and so on.

Primitive man was thus represented as childish, crude, prodigal, and comparable to animals and imbeciles. This is no exaggeration. Herbert Spencer tells us that the mind of primitive man is 'unspeculative, uncritical, incapable of generalizing, and with scarcely any notions save those yielded by the perceptions'.[3] Then, again, he says that in the undeveloped vocabularies and grammatical structures of

---

[1] F. Schleiter, *Religion and Culture*, 1919, p. 39.
[2] Radin, *Monotheism among Primitive Peoples*, 1954 edit., pp. 24–30.
[3] Op. cit., i. 344.

primitives only the simplest thoughts can be conveyed, so, according to an unnamed authority whom he quotes, the Zuni Indians 'require much facial contortion and bodily gesticulation to make their sentences perfectly intelligible'; and that the language of the Bushmen needs, according to another source, so many signs to eke it out that 'they are unintelligible in the dark', while the Arapahos, says a third authority, 'can hardly converse with one another in the dark'.[1] Max Müller quotes Sir Emerson Tennent to the effect that the Veddahs of Ceylon have no language: 'they mutually make themselves understood by signs, grimaces, and guttural sounds, which have little resemblance to definite words or language in general.'[2] In fact they speak Sinhalese (an Indo-European tongue). Then, does not Darwin, in a most unscientific passage, describe the people of Tierra del Fuego, a rather pleasant people according to better observers, as practically sub-human beasts,[3] and does not Galton, in an even more unscientific spirit, claim that his dog had more intelligence than the Damara (Herero) whom he met?[4] Many other examples could be cited. A superb collection of foolish, if not outrageous, observations of this sort may be found in the paper 'Aptitudes of Races'[5] by the Reverend Frederic W. Farrar, the author of *Eric, or Little by Little* and *The Life of Christ*. His dislike of, and hostility to, Negroes equals that of Kingsley. Fifty years of research have shown that such denigrations (the word in this context is etymologically ironical) were ill-informed misconceptions, or in other words so much rubbish.

All this fitted in very well with colonialist and other interests, and some were prepared to admit that some of the discredit must go to the American ethnologists who wanted an excuse for slavery, and some also to those who desired to find a missing link between men and monkeys.

Needless to say, it was held that primitive peoples must have the crudest religious conceptions, and we have had

[1] Op. cit. i. 149.
[2] *Selected Essays on Language, Mythology and Religion*, ii. 27.
[3] C. Darwin, *Voyage of the Beagle, 1831–36*, 1906 edit., chap. x.
[4] F. Galton, *Narrative of an Explorer in Tropical South Africa*, 1889 edit., p. 82.
[5] *Transactions of the Ethnological Society of London*, N.S., v (1867), pp. 115–26.

occasion to observe the various ways in which they are supposed to have reached them. This may further be illustrated in the condescending argument, once it was ascertained beyond doubt that primitive peoples, even the hunters and collectors, have gods with high moral attributes, that they must have borrowed the idea, or just the word without comprehension of its meaning, from a higher culture, from missionaries, traders, and others. Tylor asserted this, almost certainly wrongly, as Andrew Lang showed, about the Australian aboriginals.[1] Sidney Hartland was of the same opinion as Tylor.[2] Dorman, also on little evidence, says categorically of the Amerindians: 'No approach to monotheism had been made before the discovery of America by Europeans . . . .'[3] Modern research has shown that little value can be attributed to statements of this sort; but it was more or less an axiom of the time that, the simpler the technology and social structure, the more degraded the religious, and indeed any other, conceptions; and the opinionated Avebury went so far as to claim that there was no belief in gods nor any cult, and therefore on his definition no religion, among the Australians, the Tasmanians, the Andamanese, the Eskimoes, the Indians of North and South America, some Polynesians, at least some Caroline Islanders, the Hottentots, some Kaffirs of South Africa, the Foulahs of Central Africa, the Bambaras of West Africa, and the people of Damood Island.[4] The famous missionary Moffat, who excused himself for not describing the manners and customs of the Bechuanas on the grounds that to do so 'would be neither very instructive nor very edifying',[5] says that Satan has erased 'every vestige of religious impression from the minds of the Bechuanas, Hottentots, and Bushmen'.[6] It was not uncommon at the time to deny that the least culturally developed peoples had any religion at all. This was the opinion of Frazer, as we have earlier noted; and even as

[1] Tylor, 'On the Limits of Savage Religion', *J.A.I.*, xxi (1892), pp. 293 ff.
[2] E. S. Hartland, 'The "High Gods" of Australia', *Folk-lore*, ix (1898), p. 302.
[3] R. M. Dorman, *The Origin of Primitive Superstitions*, 1881, p. 15.
[4] Op. cit., chaps. 5 and 6.
[5] R. Moffat, *Missionary Labours and Scenes in Southern Africa*, 1842, p. 249.
[6] Ibid., p. 244. See also pp. 260–3.

late as 1928 we find Charles Singer denying that savages have anything which can be called a religious system, for their practices and beliefs totally lack coherence.[1] What he means is, I suppose, that they do not have a philosophy of religion or theological apologetics. It may, indeed, be true that primitive beliefs are vague and uncertain, but it does not seem to have occurred to these writers that so are those of ordinary peoples in our own society; for how could it be otherwise when religion concerns beings which cannot be directly apprehended by the senses or fully comprehended by reason? And if their religious myths appear sometimes to be ludicrous, they are not more so than those of Greece and Rome and India, so much admired by classical scholars and Orientalists; nor, it could be held, are their gods nearly so revolting.

Such views as I have outlined would not be acceptable today. On whether they were justified by the information available at the time I will pronounce no judgement, not having carried out the laborious literary research that would be required to form one. My task is expository, but I have also to put before you what seems to me to be the fundamental weakness of the interpretations of primitive religion which at one time appeared to carry conviction. The first error was the basing of them on evolutionary assumptions for which no evidence was, or could be, adduced. The second was that, besides being theories of chronological origins, they were also theories of psychological origins; and even those we have labelled sociological could be said to rest ultimately on psychological suppositions of the 'if I were a horse' sort. They could scarcely have been otherwise so far as the armchair anthropologists were concerned, those whose experience was restricted to their own culture and society, within that society to a small class, and within that class to a yet smaller group of intellectuals. I am sure that men like Avebury, Frazer, and Marett had little idea of how the ordinary English working man felt and thought, and it is not surprising that they had even less idea of how primitives, whom they had never

---

[1] C. Singer, *Religion and Science*, 1928, p. 7.

seen, feel and think. As we have seen, their explanations of primitive religion derived from introspection. If the scholar himself believed what primitives believe, or practised what they practise, he would have been guided by a certain line of reasoning, or impelled by some emotional state, or immersed in crowd psychology, or entangled in a network of collective and mystical representations.

How often have we been warned not to try to interpret the thought of ancient or primitive peoples in terms of our own psychology, which has been moulded by a set of institutions very different from theirs—by Adam Ferguson, Sir Henry Maine, and others, including Lévy-Bruhl, who in this respect might be said to be the most objective of all the writers about primitive mentality whose works we have reviewed. 'German scholars', Bachofen wrote to Morgan, 'propose to make antiquity intelligible by measuring it according to the popular ideas of the present day. They only see themselves in the creation of the past. To penetrate to the structure of a mind different from our own, is hardy work.'[1] It is indeed hardy work, especially when we are dealing with such difficult subjects as primitive magic and religion, in which it is all too easy, when translating the conceptions of the simpler peoples into our own, to transplant our thought into theirs. If it be true, as the Seligmans have said, that in the matter of magic black and white peoples regard each other with total lack of understanding,[2] primitive man's ideas about it are liable to be gravely distorted, especially by those who have never seen a primitive people and who also regard magic as a futile superstition. The phenomenon then tends to be analysed by the process of imagining ourselves in the same conditions as primitive man.

As I indicated in my first lecture, I regard this problem of translation as being central to our discipline. I give one more example. We use the word 'supernatural' when speaking of some native belief, because that is what it would mean for us, but far from increasing our understanding of it, we

[1] C. Resek, *Lewis Henry Morgan: American Scholar*, 1960, p. 136.
[2] C. G. and B. Z. Seligman, *Pagan Tribes of the Nilotic Sudan*, 1932, p. 25.

are likely by the use of this word to misunderstand it. We have the concept of natural law, and the word 'supernatural' conveys to us something outside the ordinary operation of cause and effect, but it may not at all have that sense for primitive man. For instance, many peoples are convinced that deaths are caused by witchcraft. To speak of witchcraft being for these peoples a supernatural agency hardly reflects their own view of the matter, since from their point of view nothing could be more natural. They experience it through the senses in deaths and other misfortunes, and the witches are their neighbours. Indeed, for them, if a person did not die from witchcraft, it might be better said, at least in a certain sense, that he did not die a natural death, and that to die from witchcraft is to die from natural causes. We might here consider further the dichotomy between sacred and profane, also the meaning of *mana* and similar ideas, the differences between magic and religion, and other topics which appear to me to be still in a very confused state, largely on account of failure to realize that very fundamental semantic problems confront us—or, if we prefer to say so, problems of translation; but this would require a lengthy discussion, to which I hope to give attention at another time and in another place.

I will only draw passing attention again to the appalling fog of confusion, which lasted for many years and is not yet entirely dispersed, about the (mainly Polynesian) concept of *mana*, a confusion partly due to the uncertain reports received from Melanesia and Polynesia and more so to the speculations of such influential writers as Marett and Durkheim, who conceived of it as a vague, impersonal force, a sort of ether or electricity which was distributed in persons and things. More recent research seems to have established that it should be understood as an efficaciousness (with the allied meaning of truth) of spiritual power derived from gods or ghosts, usually through persons, especially chiefs—a grace or virtue which enables persons to ensure success in human undertakings, and which thus corresponds to similar ideas in many parts of the world.[1]

[1] Hocart, 'Mana', *Man*, 1914, 46; 'Mana again', *Man*, 1922, 79. Firth,

Here and now I have a different task to perform: to suggest what should be the procedure in investigations of primitive religions. I do not deny that peoples have reasons for their beliefs—that they are rational; I do not deny that religious rites may be accompanied by emotional experiences, that feeling may even be an important element in their performance; and I certainly do not deny that religious ideas and practices are directly associated with social groups— that religion, whatever else it may be, is a social phenomenon. What I do deny is that it is explained by any of these facts, or all of them together, and I hold that it is not sound scientific method to seek for origins, especially when they cannot be found. Science deals with relations, not with origins and essences. In so far as it can be said that the facts of primitive religions can be sociologically explained at all, it must be in relation to other facts, both those with which it forms a system of ideas and practices and other social phenomena associated with it. As an example of the first kind of partial explanation, I would instance magic. To try to understand magic as an idea in itself, what is the essence of it, as it were, is a hopeless task. It becomes more intelligible when it is viewed not only in relation to empirical activities but also in relation to other beliefs, as part of a system of thought; for it is certainly often the case that it is primarily not so much a means of controlling nature as of preventing witchcraft and other mystical forces operating against human endeavour by interfering with the empirical measures taken to attain an end. As an example of explanation in terms of the relation of religion to other social, and in themselves non-religious, facts, we might instance ancestor cults, which clearly can only be understood when they are viewed as part of a whole set of family and kin relationships. The ghosts have power over their descendants, among whom they act as sanction for conduct, seeing that they carry out their obligations to one another and punishing them if they fail to do so. Or again,

'The Analysis of Mana: an Empirical Approach', *Journal of the Polynesian Society,* xlix (1940), pp. 483–610. A. Capell, 'The Word "Mana": a Linguistic Study', *Oceania,* ix (1938), pp. 89–96. Also, F. R. Lehmann, *Mana, Der Begriff des 'außerordentlich Wirkungsvollen' bei Südseevölkern,* 1922, *passim.*

in some societies God is conceived of as both the one and the many, the one as thought of in relation to all men or a total society, and the many as thought of, in the form of a variety of spirits, in relation to one or other segment of society. A knowledge of the social structure is here obviously required for the understanding of some features of religious thought. Then again, religious ritual is performed on ceremonial occasions in which the relative status of individuals and groups is affirmed or confirmed, as at birth, initiation, marriage, and death. Clearly, to understand the role of religion on these occasions one must here again have a knowledge of the social structure. I have given some very simple examples. A relational analysis of the kind suggested can be made at any point where religion is in a functional relation to any other social facts—moral, ethical, economic, juridical, aesthetic, and scientific—and when it has been made at all points, we have as full a sociological understanding of the phenomenon as we are ever likely to have.

All this amounts to saying that we have to account for religious facts in terms of the totality of the culture and society in which they are found, to try to understand them in terms of what the *Gestalt* psychologists called the *Kulturganze*, or of what Mauss called *fait total*. They must be seen as a relation of parts to one another within a coherent system, each part making sense only in relation to the others, and the system itself making sense only in relation to other institutional systems, as part of a wider set of relations.

I regret to say that very little progress has been made along these lines. As I have earlier remarked, when the religious crisis passed, interest among anthropologists in primitive religions dwindled, and between the end of the First World War and recently there was a dearth of studies on the subject by those who had done field research. Perhaps, also, field research into this particular topic demands a poetic mind which moves easily in images and symbols. So while in other departments of anthropology some, even considerable, advance has been made by intensive research, in the study of kinship and of political institutions for example, I do not think that comparable advance has been made in the study of primitive religion. Religion is, of course, expressed in ritual, and it is a symptom of the lack of interest shown in recent years that it has been noted that, of the ninety-nine publications of the Rhodes–Livingstone Institute dealing with various aspects of African life during the last thirty or so years, only three have taken ritual for their subject.[1] I am glad to say, however, since primitive religion in a broad sense has been one of my own chief interests, that lately there have been signs of a renewed interest in it, and from what we have called a relational point of view. I do not wish to be selective, but I might cite as examples a few recent books on African religions: Dr. Godfrey Lienhardt's *Divinity and Experience*, an analytical study of the religion of the Dinka of the Sudan,[2] Dr. John Middleton's study of the religious conceptions and rites of the Lugbara people of Uganda,[3] and Dr. Victor Turner's study of Ndembu ritual and symbolism in Northern Rhodesia;[4] and also, outside our professional ranks, such researches as those of Fr. Tempels[5] and Fr. Theuws[6] among the Baluba of the Congo. These recent researches in particular societies bring us nearer to the formulation of the problem of what is the part played by religion, and in general by what might be called non-scientific thought, in social life.

Now, sooner or later, if we are to have a general sociological theory of religion, we shall have to take into consideration all religions and not just primitive religions; and only by so doing can we understand some of its essential features. For as the advances of science and technology have rendered magic redundant, religion has persisted, and its social role has become ever more embracing, involving persons more and more remote and no longer, as in primitive societies, bound by ties of family and kin and participating in corporate activities.

[1] R. Apthorpe, introduction to 'Elements in Luvale Beliefs and Rituals', by C. M. N. White, *Rhodes–Livingstone Papers*, no. 32 (1961), p. ix.

[2] G. Lienhardt, *Divinity and Experience. The Religion of the Dinka*, 1961.

[3] J. Middleton, *Lugbara Religion*, 1960.

[4] V. W. Turner, 'Ndembu Divination: its Symbolism and Techniques', *Rhodes–Livingstone Papers*, no. 31 (1961): 'Ritual Symbolism, Morality and Social Structure among the Ndembu', *Rhodes–Livingstone Journal*, no. 30 (1961).

[5] R. P. Placide Tempels, *Bantu Philosophy*, 1959.

[6] Th. Theuws, 'Le Réel dans la conception Luba', *Zaïre*, xv (1961), 1.

If we do not have some general statements to make about religion, we do not go beyond innumerable particular studies of the religions of particular peoples. During last century such general statements were indeed attempted, as we have seen, in the form of evolutionary and psychological and sociological hypotheses, but since these attempts at general formulations seem to have been abandoned by anthropologists, our subject has suffered from loss of common aim and method. The so-called functional method was too vague and too slick to persist, and also too much coloured by pragmatism and teleology. It rested too much on a rather flimsy biological analogy; and little was done by comparative research to support conclusions reached in particular studies—indeed, comparative studies were becoming almost obsolete.

Several philosophers and near-philosophers have attempted to set forth in the broadest possible way what they conceived to be the role of religion in social life, and I now turn to see what we may learn from them. In spite of all his plagiarism, his prolixity, and his triviality, Pareto saw, as we have already observed, that non-logical ways of thought, that is, actions (and the ideas associated with them) in which means are not, from the standpoint of experimental science, rationally adapted to ends, play an essential part in social relations; and in that category he placed religion. Prayer may be efficacious, though Pareto obviously did not himself think so, but its efficacy is not accepted by the consensus of scientific opinion as fact. Where technical precision of one sort or another is necessary, as in science, military operations, law, and politics, reason must dominate. Otherwise, in our social relations and in the sphere of our values and affections and loyalties, sentiment prevails: in our attachment to family and home, to church and state, and in our conduct to our fellows; and these sentiments are of the utmost importance, among them being the religious sentiments. In other words, certain activities require strictly rational thought—using 'rational' here as shorthand for his 'logico-experimental'—but they can only be carried out if there is also some measure of solidarity between the persons involved and security and order, and these depend on common sentiments, which derive from moral, not technical, needs, and are based on imperatives and axioms and not on observation and experiment. They are constructs of the heart rather than of the mind, which here serves only to find reasons to protect them. Hence Pareto's aim, cited earlier, to demonstrate experimentally 'the individual and social utility of non-logical conduct'.[1] I think he was trying to say that in the realm of values only the means are chosen by reason, not the ends, a view shared, among others, by Aristotle and Hume.

To take another example, the philosopher Henri Bergson was, though in a different manner, making the same distinction between the two broad types of thought and behaviour, the religious and the scientific. We must study them in action; and also, we must not be led astray by Lévy-Bruhl into supposing that, in bringing in mystical causes, primitive man is thereby explaining physical effects; rather, he is accounting for their human significance, their significance for him. The difference between savages and ourselves is simply that we have more scientific knowledge than they have: they 'are ignorant of what we have learnt'.[2]

Bearing these comments in mind, we turn to Bergson's main thesis. Fundamentally, he says, human society and culture serve a biological purpose, and the two types of mental function serve this purpose in different ways and are complementary. There are two different sorts of religious experience, the static, that associated with the closed society, and the dynamic or mystical (in the individualist sense that the word has in historical writings and comparative studies of religion, and not in Lévy-Bruhl's sense), which is associated with the open, the universal, society. The former is, of course, characteristic of primitive societies. Now, biological evolution, with regard to both structure and organization, has taken two directions: towards the perfection of instinct in the whole animal kingdom except for man, and towards the perfection of intelligence in man alone. If intelligence has its advantages, it has also its disadvantages. Unlike animals, primitive man can foresee the difficulties before him and has

---

[1] *The Mind and Society*, p. 35.   [2] Bergson, op. cit., p. 151.

doubts and fears about his ability to overcome them. Yet action is imperative. Above all, he knows that he must die. This realization of helplessness inhibits action and imperils life. Reflection, the pale cast of thought, has another danger. Societies persist because of a sense of moral obligation among their members; but his intelligence may tell a man that his own selfish interests should come first, whether they conflict with the general good or not.

Confronted with these dilemmas, Nature (these reifications abound in Bergson's writings) makes an adjustment to restore man's confidence and impose his sacrifice by delving into the instinctual depths covered over by the layer of intelligence. With the myth-making faculty she finds there she puts his intelligence to sleep, though without destroying it. From it are derived magic and religion, at first undifferentiated, though later each goes its own way. They supply the necessary balance to intelligence and allow man, by manipulating imaginary forces in nature or by appealing to imaginary spirits, to turn again towards his goal; and they compel him also to forget his selfish interests in the common interest and to submit, through taboos, to social discipline. So, what instinct does for animals, religion does for man, by aiding his intelligence in opposing to it in critical situations intellectual representations. Therefore religion is not, as some have supposed, a product of fear, but an assurance, and insurance, against fear. Ultimately it is a product of an instinctual urge, a vital impulse which, combined with intelligence, ensures man's survival and his evolutionary climb to ever greater heights. In a sentence, it is, says Bergson, 'a defensive reaction of nature against the dissolvent power of intelligence'.[1] So, since these functions of religion, in whatever monstrous constructs of the imagination it may proliferate, not being anchored to reality, are essential for survival, both of the person and of society, we need not be surprised that while there have been, and are, societies which lack science, art, and philosophy, there never has been one without religion. 'Religion, being co-extensive with our species, must pertain to our structure.'[2]

---

[1] Op. cit., p. 122.   [2] Ibid., p. 176.

Bergson made use of secondary sources, particularly the writings of his friend Lévy-Bruhl, when he wrote about primitive ideas in contemporaneous simple societies, but when he spoke of primitive man he had in mind some hypothetical prehistoric man, and this man was more or less a dialectical device to enable him to make a stronger contrast between the static religion of the closed society and the mystical religion of the open society of the future which his imagination, guided by personal religious experience, envisaged.

You may have noted that in a very general way Bergson's 'instinct' corresponds to Pareto's 'non-logico-experimental residues' and to Lévy-Bruhl's 'pre-logical', and his 'intelligence' to Pareto's 'logico-experimental' and to Lévy-Bruhl's 'logical'; and that the problem seen by Pareto and Bergson but not, I think, by Lévy-Bruhl, was, though from different points of view, much the same. It may further be observed that while all three tell us much about the nature of the irrational, they tell us very little about the rational, and therefore one is not quite sure in what the differences in the contrast consist.

The German social historian Max Weber,[1] to take a final example, touches on the same problem, though not so explicitly; and his 'rational' as against the 'traditional' and 'charismatic' to some degree corresponds to the opposed terms of the other writers. He distinguishes these three ideal or 'pure' types of social activity. The rational is the most intelligible type, best observed in the capitalist economics of the West, though evident in all activities subject to bureaucratic control, routinization, and their product, almost complete depersonalization. The traditional is characterized by piety for what has always existed, typical of conservative and relatively changeless societies in which affective, or affectual, sentiments predominate. Primitive societies belong to this type, though he appears to have read little about them. The charismatic, until it becomes routinized by banausic officialdom, as it inevitably does if it is successful, is the free, individual, emergence of the spirit: it is represented by the

[1] *From Max Weber: Essays in Sociology*, 1947.

prophet, the heroic warrior, the revolutionary, &c., who appear as leaders in times of distress, and are credited with extraordinary and supernatural gifts. Such leaders may appear in any society.

Like Bergson, Max Weber distinguishes between what he calls magical religiosity, the religions of primitive and barbarous peoples, and the universalist religions of the prophets who shattered the mystical (in his sense of the word) ties of the closed society, of the exclusive groups and associations of community life; though both alike are mostly concerned with this-worldly values: health, long life, and wealth. In one sense of the word, religion is not in itself non-rational. Puritanism and apologetics and casuistry are highly rational. This being so, it follows that doctrines may create an ethos conducive to secular developments: the Protestant sects and the rise of Western capitalism are an example. But it is nevertheless in tension with secular rationality, which slowly ousts it from one sphere after another—law, politics, economics, and science—and so this leads, in Friedrich Schiller's phrase, to the 'disenchantment of the world'. In another sense, therefore, religion is non-rational, even in its rationalized forms; and although Max Weber saw it as a refuge from the complete destruction of the personality by the inevitable trends of modern life, he could not himself take shelter in it: one must rather accept imprisonment in a terrible society and be prepared to be a cog in a machine, depriving oneself of all that it means to be an individual who has personal relations with other individuals. But, though things are moving in that direction, religion still plays an important part in social life, and it is the role of the sociologist to show what that part is, not only in the rationalized societies of Western Europe but also in earlier periods of history and in other parts of the world, demonstrating how, in different types of society, different types of religion both shaped, and were shaped by, other areas of social life. In brief, we have to ask what is the role of the non-rational in social life and what parts are, and have been, played in that life by the rational, the traditional, and the charismatic. He is asking much the same questions as Pareto and Bergson.

Such are the questions—I give no more examples. Are the answers to them any more satisfactory than those we have considered in earlier lectures? I think not. They are too vague, too general, a bit too easy, and they smell strongly of pragmatist special pleading. Religion helps to preserve social cohesion, it gives men confidence, and so on. But do such explanations take us very far, and if they are true, which has to be proved, how does one set about determining in what way and in what degree does religion have these effects?

My answer to the question I have asked must be that I think that while the problem posed is, wide though it may be, a real one, the answers are not impressive. I would propose instead that we do some research into the matter. Comparative religion is a subject hardly represented in our universities, and the data of what claims to be such are derived almost entirely from books—sacred texts, theological writings, exegetics, mystical writings, and all the rest of it. But for the anthropologist or sociologist, I would suggest, this is perhaps the least significant part of religion, especially as it is very evident that the scholars who write books on the historical religions are sometimes uncertain what even key words meant to the authors of the original texts. The philological reconstructions and interpretations of these key words are only too often uncertain, contradictory, and unconvincing, e.g. in the case of the word 'god'. The student of an ancient religion or of a religion in its early phases has no other means of examining it than in texts, for the people contemporaneous with the texts are no more and cannot therefore be consulted. Serious distortions may result, as when it is said that Buddhism and Jainism are atheistic religions. No doubt they may have been regarded as systems of philosophy and psychology by the authors of the systems but we may well ask whether they were by ordinary people; and it is ordinary people the anthropologist is chiefly interested in. To him what is most important is how religious beliefs and practices affect in any society the minds, the feelings, the lives, and the inter-relations of its members. There are few books which describe and analyse in any adequate manner the role of religion in any Hindu, Buddhist, Moslem, or Christian community.

For the social anthropologist, religion is what religion does. I must add that such studies among primitive peoples have been few and far between. In both civilized and primitive societies herein lies an enormous and almost untilled field for research.

Furthermore, comparative religion must be comparative in a relational manner if much that is worth while is to come out of the exercise. If comparison is to stop at mere description—Christians believe this, Moslems that, and Hindus the other—or even if it goes a step further and classifies—Zoroastrianism, Judaism, and Islam are prophetic religions, Hinduism and Buddhism are mystical religions (or, certain religions are world-accepting while others are world-denying)—we are not taken very far towards an understanding of either similarities or differences. The Indian monists, the Buddhists, and the Manichees may all be alike in desiring release from the body and detachment from the world of sense, but the question we would ask is whether this common element is related to any other social facts. An attempt was made in this direction by Weber and Tawney[1] in relating certain Protestant teachings to certain economic changes. Indeed, far be it from me to belittle students of comparative religion on this score, for, as I hope I have shown in earlier lectures, we anthropologists have not made much progress in the sort of relational studies which I believe to be those required and the only ones which are likely to lead us to a vigorous sociology of religion.

Indeed, I have to conclude that I do not feel that on the whole the different theories we have reviewed, either singly or taken together, give us much more than common-sense guesses, which for the most part miss the mark. If we ask ourselves, as we naturally do, whether they have any bearing on our own religious experience—whether, shall we say, they make any more significant for us 'Peace I leave you, my peace I give unto you . . .'—I suppose that the answer must be that they have little, and this may make us sceptical about their value as explanations of the religions of primitives,

---

[1] M. Weber, *The Protestant Ethic and the Spirit of Capitalism*, 1930; R. H. Tawney, *Religion and the Rise of Capitalism*, 1944 edit.

who cannot apply the same test. The reason for this is, I believe, partly one I have already given, that the writers were
seeking for explanations in terms of origins and essences
instead of relations; and I would further suggest that this
followed from their assumptions that the souls and spirits and
gods of religion have no reality. For if they are regarded as
complete illusions, then some biological, psychological, or
sociological theory of how everywhere and at all times men
have been stupid enough to believe in them seems to be
called for. He who accepts the reality of spiritual being does
not feel the same need for such explanations, for, inadequate
though the conceptions of soul and God may be among
primitive peoples, they are not just an illusion for him. As
far as a study of religion as a factor in social life is concerned,
it may make little difference whether the anthropologist is a
theist or an atheist, since in either case he can only take into
account what he can observe. But if either attempts to go
further than this, each must pursue a different path. The
non-believer seeks for some theory—biological, psychological,
or sociological—which will explain the illusion; the believer
seeks rather to understand the manner in which a people
conceives of a reality and their relations to it. For both,
religion is part of social life, but for the believer it has also
another dimension. On this point I find myself in agreement
with Schmidt in his confutation of Renan: 'If religion is
essentially of the inner life, it follows that it can be truly
grasped only from within. But beyond a doubt, this can be
better done by one in whose inward consciousness an experience of religion plays a part. There is but too much
danger that the other [the non-believer] will talk of religion
as a blind man might of colours, or one totally devoid of ear,
of a beautiful musical composition.'[1]

In these lectures I have given you an account of some of
the main past attempts at explaining primitive religions, and
I have asked you to accept that none of them is wholly
satisfactory. We seem always to have come out by the same
door as we went in. But I would not wish to have you believe
that so much labour has been to no purpose. If we are now

[1] W. Schmidt, *The Origin and Growth of Religion*, 1931, p. 6.

able to see the errors in these theories purporting to account for primitive religions, it is partly because they were set forth, thereby inviting logical analysis of their contents and the testing of them against recorded ethnological fact and in field research. The advance in this department of social anthropology in the last forty or so years may be measured by the fact that, in the light of the knowledge we now have, we can point to the inadequacies of theories which at one time carried conviction, but we might never have obtained this knowledge had it not been for the pioneers whose writings we have reviewed.

BIBLIOGRAPHY

ALLIER, RAOUL. *Les Non-civilisés et nous*, 1927.

ATKINSON, J. J. *Primal Law* in *Social Origins* by Andrew Lang, 1903.

AVEBURY, RT. HON. LORD. *Marriage, Totemism and Religion. An Answer to Critics*, 1911.

BAKER, SIR SAMUEL. 'The Races of the Nile Basin', *Transactions of the Ethnological Society of London*, N.S., vol. v, 1867.

BEATTIE, JOHN. *Other Cultures*, 1964.

BENEDICT, RUTH. 'Religion' in Franz Boas and others, *General Anthropology*, 1938.

BERGSON, HENRI. *The Two Sources of Morality and Religion*, 1956 edit. (First pub. in France in 1932.)

BLEEKER, C. J. *The Sacred Bridge*, 1963.

BOAS, FRANZ. *The Mind of Primitive Man*, 1911.

BORKENAU, FRANZ. *Pareto*, 1936.

BOUSQUET, G. H. *Précis de sociologie d'après Vilfredo Pareto*, 1925.

—— *Vilfredo Pareto, sa vie et son œuvre*, 1928.

BUBER, MARTIN. *Between Man and Man*, 1961 edit. (First pub. 1947.)

BUKHARIN, NIKOLAI. *Historical Materialism. A System of Sociology*, 1925.

CAPELL, A. 'The Word "Mana": a Linguistic Study', *Oceania*, vol. ix, 1938.

CLODD, EDWARD. *Tom Tit Tot*, 1898.

—— 'Presidential Address', *Folk-lore*, vol. vii, 1896.

COMTE, AUGUSTE. *Cours de philosophie positive*, 1908 edit., vols. iv–vi. (First pub. 1830–42.)

CORNFORD, F. M. *From Religion to Philosophy*, 1912.

CRAWLEY, A. E. *The Mystic Rose*, 1927 edit. (revised and enlarged by Theodore Besterman), 2 vols. (First pub. in 1902.)

—— *The Tree of Life*, 1905.

—— *The Idea of the Soul*, 1909.

CROOKE, W. 'Method of Investigation and Folk-lore Origin', *Folk-lore*, vol. xxiv, 1913.

DARWIN, CHARLES ROBERT. *Voyage of the Beagle, 1831–36*, 1906 edit. (First pub. in 1839.)

DAVY, GEORGES. *Sociologues d'hier et d'aujourd'hui*, 1931.

DE BROSSES, CH. R. *Du Culte des dieux fétiches ou parallèle de l'ancienne religion de l'Egypte avec la religion actuelle de la Nigritie*, 1760.

DORMAN, RUSHTON M. *The Origin of Primitive Superstitions*, 1881.

DRIBERG, J. H. *The Savage as he really is*, 1929.

—— *At Home with the Savage*, 1932.

DURKHEIM, E. 'De la définition des phénomènes religieux', *L'Année sociologique*, vol. ii, 1899.

DURKHEIM, E. *Les Formes élémentaires de la vie religieuse*, 1912 (Eng. trans. *The Elementary Forms of the Religious Life*, n.d. [1915]).

ESSERTIER, D. *Philosophes et savants français du XXᵉ siècle, la sociologie*, 1930.

EVANS-PRITCHARD, E. E. 'Heredity and Gestation as the Azande see them', *Sociologus*, 1931. (Reprinted in *Essays in Social Anthropology*, 1962.)

—— 'The Intellectualist (English) Interpretation of Magic', *Bulletin of the Faculty of Arts*, Egyptian University (Cairo), vol. i, 1933.

—— 'Lévy-Bruhl's Theory of Primitive Mentality', *Bulletin of the Faculty of Arts*, Egyptian University (Cairo), vol. ii, 1934.

—— 'Zande Therapeutics', *Essays presented to C. G. Seligman*, 1934.

—— 'Science and Sentiment. An Exposition and Criticism of the Writings of Pareto', *Bulletin of the Faculty of Arts*, Egyptian University (Cairo), vol. iii, 1936.

—— *Witchcraft, Oracles and Magic among the Azande*, 1937.

—— 'Obituary: Lucien Lévy-Bruhl, 1939', *Man*, 1940, no. 27.

—— *Nuer Religion*, 1956.

—— 'Religion and the Anthropologist', *Blackfriars*, April 1960. (Reprinted in *Essays in Social Anthropology*, 1962.)

FARNELL, L. R. *The Evolution of Religion*, 1905.

FARRAR, THE REVD. F. W. 'Aptitudes of Races', *Transactions of the Ethnological Society of London*, N.S., vol. v, 1867.

FIRTH, RAYMOND. 'The Analysis of Mana: an empirical Approach', *Journal of the Polynesian Society*, vol. xlix, no. 196, 1940.

—— 'Magic, Primitive', *Encyclopaedia Britannica*, 1955 edit., vol. xiv.

FLUGEL, J. C. *A Hundred Years of Psychology, 1833–1933*, 1933.

FORTUNE, R. F. *Sorcerers of Dobu*, 1932.

FRAZER, J. G. *Psyche's Task*, 1913.

—— *The Golden Bough*, 3rd edit., 1922, 2 vols. (First pub. in 1890.)

—— *The Gorgon's Head*, 1927.

FREUD, SIGMUND. *Totem and Taboo*, n.d. (First pub. in German in 1913.)

—— *The Future of an Illusion*, 1928.

FUSTEL DE COULANGES, N. D. *The Ancient City*, 4th edit. (1882). (First pub. in France, *La Cité antique*, in 1864).

GALTON, FRANCIS. *Narrative of an Explorer in Tropical South Africa*, 1889 edit. (First pub. in 1853.)

GINSBERG, MORRIS. *Essays in Sociology and Social Philosophy*, vol. iii. *Evolution and Progress*, 1961.

GOLDENWEISER, ALEXANDER A. 'Religion and Society: A Critique of Émile Durkheim's Theory of the Origin and Nature of Religion', *Journal of Philosophy, Psychology and Scientific Methods*, vol. xii, 1917.

—— 'Form and Content in Totemism', *American Anthropologist*, N.S., vol. xx, 1918.

—— *Early Civilization*, 1921.

HADDON, A. C. *Magic and Fetishism*, 1906.

HARRISON, JANE ELLEN. *Themis. A Study of the Social Origins of Greek Religion*, 1912.

HARTLAND, E. SIDNEY. *The Legend of Perseus*, 3 vols., 1894–6.

—— 'The "High Gods" of Australia', *Folk-lore*, vol. ix, 1898.

HEILER, FRIEDRICH. *Das Gebet*, 1919.

HENDERSON, L. J. *Pareto's General Sociology. A Physiologist's Interpretation*, 1935.

HERTZ, ROBERT. *Death and the Right Hand*, 1960. (First pub. in France in 1907 and 1909.)

HOCART, A. M. 'Mana', *Man*, 1914, 46.

—— 'Mana again', *Man*, 1922, 79.

—— *The Progress of Man*, 1933.

HOGBIN, H. IAN. 'Mana', *Oceania*, vol. vi, no. 3, 1936.

HOMANS, G. C., and CURTIS, C. P. *An Introduction to Pareto. His Sociology*, 1934.

HUBERT, H., and MAUSS, M. 'Essai sur la nature et la fonction du sacrifice', *L'Année sociologique*, vol. ii, 1899.

—— 'Esquisse d'une théorie générale de la magie', *L'Année sociologique*, vol. vii, 1904.

—— *Mélanges d'histoire des religions*, 2nd edit., 1929.

HUME, DAVID. *The Natural History of Religion*, 1956 edit. (First pub., 1757.)

JAMES, E. O. *Primitive Ritual and Belief*, 1917.

JAMES, WILLIAM. *The Principles of Psychology*, 1890.

—— *The Varieties of Religious Experience*, 13th impr., 1907. (First pub. in 1902.)

—— *Pragmatism and four Essays from the Meaning of Truth*, 1959 edit. (First pub. in 1907 and 1909.)

JEVONS, F. B. 'Report on Greek Mythology', *Folk-lore*, vol. ii, no. 2, pp. 220–41, 1891.

—— *An Introduction to the History of Religion*, 9th edit., n.d. (First pub. in 1896.)

—— *An Introduction to the Study of Comparative Religion*, 1908.

KING, JOHN H. *The Supernatural: its Origin, Nature, and Evolution*, 2 vols., 1892.

KISHIMOTO, HIDEO. 'An Operational Definition of Religion', *Numen*, Dec. 1961.

KROEBER, A. L. *The Religion of the Indians of California*, University of California Publications, vol. iv, 1907.

LALANDE, ANDRÉ. *Vocabulaire technique et critique de la philosophie*, art. 'Logique'. 1932.

LANG, ANDREW. *The Making of Religion*, 1898.

—— 'Are Savage Gods borrowed from Missionaries?', *The Nineteenth Century*, Jan. 1899.

—— *Social Origins*, 1903.

LEHMANN, F. R. *Mana, Der Begriff des 'außerordentlich Wirkungsvollen' bei Südseevölkern*, 1922.

LEROY, OLIVIER. *La Raison primitive, Essai de réfutation de la théorie de prélogisme*, 1927.

LEUBA, JAMES H. *A Psychological Study of Religion, its Origin, Function and Future*, 1912.

LÉVI-STRAUSS, CLAUDE, *Totemism*, 1963 (*Le Totémisme aujourd'hui*, 1962).

LÉVY-BRUHL, LUCIEN. *La Morale et la science des mœurs*, 3rd edit., 1937. (Eng. trans. *Ethics and Moral Science*, 1905.)

—— *Les Fonctions mentales dans les sociétés inférieures*, 2nd edit., 1912. (First pub. 1910: Eng. trans. *How Natives Think*, 1926.)

—— *La Mentalité primitive*, 14th edit., 1947. (First pub. in 1922: Eng. trans. *Primitive Mentality*, 1923.)

—— *L'Âme primitive*, 1927. (Eng. trans. *The Soul of the Primitive*, 1928.)

—— *La Mentalité primitive* (The Herbert Spencer Lecture), 1931.

—— *Le Surnaturel et la nature dans la mentalité primitive*, 1931. (Eng. trans. *Primitives and the Supernatural*, 1936.)

—— *L'Expérience mystique et les symboles chez les primitifs*, 1938.

—— *Les Carnets de Lucien Lévy-Bruhl*, 1949.

—— 'Une Lettre de Lucien Lévy-Bruhl au Professeur Evans-Pritchard', *Revue philosophique*, no. 4, 1957. ('A Letter to E. E. Evans-Pritchard, *The British Journal of Sociology*, vol. iii, 1952.)

LIENHARDT, GODFREY. *Divinity and Experience. The Religion of the Dinka*, 1961.

LOISY, ALFRED. *Essai historique sur le sacrifice*, 1920.

LOWIE, ROBERT H. *Primitive Society*, 1921.

—— *Primitive Religion*, 1925.

MAINE, SIR HENRY SUMNER. *Ancient Law*, 1912 edit. (First pub. 1861.)

MALINOWSKI, BRONISLAW. 'The Economic Aspect of the Intichiuma Ceremonies', *Festskrift Tillëgnad Edvard Westermarck*, 1912.

—— 'Baloma; the Spirits of the Dead in the Trobriand Islands', *Journal of the Royal Anthropological Institute*, vol. xlvi, 1916.

—— *Argonauts of the Western Pacific*, 1922.

—— 'Magic, Science and Religion', *Science, Religion and Reality*, 1925 (ed. J. A. Needham).

—— *Crime and Custom in Savage Society*, 1926.

MARETT, R. R. *The Threshold of Religion*, 2nd edit., 1914. (First pub. in 1909.)

—— *Anthropology*, 1912.

—— 'Magic', in Hastings' *Encyclopaedia of Religion and Ethics*, vol. viii, 1915.

—— *Psychology and Folk-lore*, 1920.

——*The Raw Material of Religion*, 1929.

—— *Faith, Hope and Charity in Primitive Religion*, 1932.

—— 'Religion (Primitive Religion)', *Encyclopaedia Britannica*, 11th edit., vol. xxiii.

MAUSS, M. 'Essai sur les variations saisonnières des sociétés eskimos. Étude de morphologie sociale', *L'Année sociologique*, vol. ix, 1906.

—— *Bulletin de la Société Française de Philosophie*, 1923.

McLENNAN, J. F. *Studies in Ancient History, The Second Series*, 1896.

MIDDLETON, JOHN. *Lugbara Religion*, 1960.

MOFFAT, R. *Missionary Labours and Scenes in Southern Africa*, 1842.

MONTESQUIEU, M. DE SECONDAT, BARON DE. *The Spirit of Laws*, 2 vols., 1750. (First pub. in French, *L'Esprit des lois*, in 1748.)

MÜLLER, F. MAX. *Lectures on the Origin and Growth of Religion*, 1878.
—— *Selected Essays on Language, Mythology and Religion*, 2 vols., 1881.
—— *Introduction to the Science of Religion*, 1882.
—— *Chips from a German Workshop. Essays on Mythology and Folk-lore*, vol. iv, 1895.
—— *The Life and Letters of the Rt. Hon. Friedrich Max Müller*, edit. by his wife. 2 vols. 1902.
MYRES, J. L. 'The Methods of Magic and of Science', *Folk-lore*, vol. xxxvi, 1925.
NORBECK, EDWARD. *Religion in Primitive Society*, 1961.
OTTO, RUDOLF. *The Idea of the Holy*, 1926 impression. (First pub. in 1917: *Das Heilige*.)
PARETO, VILFREDO. *Le Mythe vertuiste et la littérature immorale*, 1911.
—— *The Mind and Society*. 4 vols., 1935. (First pub. in Italy in 1916: *Trattato di sociologia generale*, 2 vols.)
—— Address. *Journal d'Économie Politique*, 1917, pp. 426 ff. (Appendix to G. C. Homans and C. P. Curtis, *An Introduction to Pareto. His Sociology*, 1934.)
PETTAZZONI, RAFFAELE. *Essays on the History of Religions*, 1954.
—— *The All-Knowing God*, 1956. (Pub. in Italy in 1955: *L'onniscienza di Dio*.)
PREUSS, K. T. 'Der Ursprung der Religion und Kunst', *Globus*, 1904-5.
RADCLIFFE-BROWN, A. R. *The Andaman Islanders*, 1922. (First pub. under the name of Brown, A. R.)
—— 'The Sociological Theory of Totemism', *Fourth Pacific Science Congress, Java, 1929, vol. 3 Biological Papers*, pp. 295-309.
—— *Taboo*, 1939.
—— 'Religion and Society', *Journal of the Royal Anthropological Institute*, 1945.
RADIN, PAUL. *Social Anthropology*, 1932.
—— *Primitive Religion. Its Nature and Origin*, 1938.
—— *Monotheism among Primitive Peoples*, 1954 edit.
READ, CARVETH. *The Origin of Man and of his Superstitions*, 1920.
REINACH, SALOMON. *Orpheus. A History of Religions*, 1931 edit. (First pub. 1909.)
RESEK, CARL. *Lewis Henry Morgan; American Scholar*, 1960.
RIGNANO, EUGENIO. *The Psychology of Reasoning*, 1923.
RIVERS, W. H. R. *Medicine, Magic and Religion*, 1927.
ROSKOFF, GUSTAV. *Das Religionswesen der rohesten Naturvölker*, 1880.
SCHLEITER, FREDERICK. *Religion and Culture*, 1919.
SCHMIDT, WILHELM. *The Origin and Growth of Religion*, 1931.
—— *Der Ursprung der Gottesidee*. 12 vols., 1912-55.
SELIGMAN, C. G. and B. Z. *Pagan Tribes of the Nilotic Sudan*, 1932.
SINGER, CHARLES. *Religion and Science*, 1928.
SMITH, W. ROBERTSON. *The Prophets of Israel*, 1902. (First pub. 1882.)
—— *The Religion of the Semites*, 3rd edit., 1927. (First pub. 1889.)
SNAITH, NORMAN H. *The Distinctive Ideas of the Old Testament*, 1944.

SÖDERBLOM, N. *Das Werden des Gottesglaubens*, 1916.

SOROKIN, PITIRIM. *Contemporary Sociological Theories*, 1928.

SPENCER, HERBERT. *A System of Synthetic Philosophy, vol. 6. The Principles of Sociology*, vol. i, 1882.

STEINER, FRANZ. *Taboo*, 1956.

SWANSON, GUY. E. *The Birth of the Gods. The Origin of Primitive Beliefs*, 1960.

SWANTON, JOHN R. 'Some Anthropological Misconceptions', *American Anthropologist*, N.S., vol. xix, 1917.

—— 'Three Factors in Primitive Religion', *American Anthropologist*, N.S., vol. xxvi, 1924.

TAWNEY, R. H. *Religion and the Rise of Capitalism*, 1944 edit. (First pub. 1926.)

TEMPELS, R. P. PLACIDE. *Bantu Philosophy*, 1959. (Pub. in French, *La Philosophie bantoue*, in 1945.)

THEUWS, TH. 'Le Réel dans la conception Luba', *Zaïre*, vol. xv, 1, 1961.

THOMAS, N. W. 'Magic and Religion: a Criticism of Dr. Jevons' Paper', *Folk-lore*, vol. xxix, 1918.

THURNWALD, R. 'Zauber, Allgemein', *Reallexicon der Vorgeschichte*, 1929.

TROELTSCH, ERNST. *The Social Teaching of the Christian Churches*, 2 vols., 1931. (First pub. in German, 1911: *Die Soziallehren der christlichen Kirchen und Gruppen*.)

TROTTER, W. *Instincts of the Herd in Peace and War*, 5th impression, 1920. (First pub. in 1916.)

TURNER, V. W. 'Ndembu Divination: its Symbolism and Techniques', *Rhodes–Livingstone Papers*, no. 31, 1961.

—— 'Ritual Symbolism, Morality and Social Structure among the Ndembu', *Rhodes–Livingstone Journal*, no. 30, 1961.

TYLOR, EDWARD B. *Researches into the Early History of Mankind*, 2nd edit. 1870. (First pub. in 1865.)

—— *Primitive Culture*. 2 vols., 3rd edit. 1891. (First pub. in 1871.)

—— Review of Dorman, Rushton M., *The Origin of Primitive Superstitions*, *The Academy*, Sat., 5 Nov. 1881.

—— 'On the Limits of Savage Religion', *Journal of the Anthropological Institute*, vol. xxi, 1892.

VAN DER LEEUW, G. 'Le Structure de la mentalité primitive', *La Revue d'Histoire et de Philosophie Religieuse*, 1928.

—— *L'Homme primitif et la religion, étude anthropologique*, 1940.

VAN GENNEP, ARNOLD. *L'État actuel du problème totémique*, 1920.

WACH, JOACHIM. *Sociology of Religion*, 1947.

WEBB, CLEMENT C. J. *Group Theories of Religion and the Individual*, 1916.

WEBER, MAX. *The Protestant Ethic and the Spirit of Capitalism*, 1930. (First pub. under the title *Die protestantische Ethik und der Geist des Kapitalismus*, in 1904–5. *From Max Weber: Essays in Sociology*, 1947.

—— *The Religion of China: Confucianism and Taoism*, 1951.

—— *The Religion of India: The Sociology of Hinduism and Buddhism*, 1958.

WHEELER, GERALD C. *The Tribe and Intertribal Relations in Australia*, 1910.

WHITE, C. M. N. 'Elements in Luvale Beliefs and Rituals'. *Rhodes–Livingstone Papers*, no. 32, 1961.

WILLIAMSON, ROBERT W. *Religious and Cosmic Beliefs of Central Polynesia*, 2 vols., 1933.

—— *Religion and Social Organization in Central Polynesia*, 1937.

WILSON, BRYAN R. *Sects and Society. A Sociological Study of three Religious Groups in Britain*, 1961.

WORSLEY, PETER. *The Trumpet shall Sound*, 1957.

WUNDT, WILHELM. *Völkerpsychologie*, vol. ii, 1906.

—— *Elements of Folk Psychology*, 1916. (First pub. in 1912: *Elemente der Völkerpsychologie*.)

ZAEHNER, R. C. *At Sundry Times*, 1958.

INDEX